Mesothelioma is not a word that is widely known among the general public. Yet!

This asbestos related lung disease has no known cure and its diagnosis means certain, usually imminent death. Its consequences are dramatic for the sufferer. And with a rapidly growing number of claims by those whose work has brought them into direct contact with asbestos dust, the implications for the insurance industry worldwide could be catastrophic.

Brenda McKessock should know more about mesothelioma than most. Recently, Ellen McKessock, her mother, an otherwise healthy former factory worker, died of the disease after a painful illness.

The book is first and foremost an account of Ellen's suffering and death. From such poignant first hand experience, the author first became confused and angry at the levels of ignorance about her mother's disease even among the medical profession. She researched the condition and found out much more of what she needed to know.

MESOTHELIOMA
the story of an illness

MESOTHELIOMA
the story of an illness

Brenda McKessock

Argyll
publishing

First published 1995
Argyll Publishing
Glendaruel
Argyll PA22 3AE

**British Library Cataloguing-in-Publication Data.
A catalogue record for this book is available from
the British Library.**

ISBN 1 874640 21 1

Origination
Cordfall Ltd, Glasgow

Printing
Martins the Printers, Berwick upon Tweed

"No one knows what I'm going through."

Ellen McKessock, 1993

In memory of mum

Acknowledgements

WITHOUT the courage, sense of humour and love of my mother, this book would never have been written. So, although she is no longer with us, my deepest thanks go to her.

Thank you to my family—Stanley McKessock, Anne Hebburn and Ellen Gordon for their help and support. And to Callum for his patience and understanding throughout.

Very special thanks to all the people who have opened their minds and hearts to tell me their story, hard as I know this was—Trudy Phillips, Else Standen, Pat Standen, John McPherson, Nan McKenzie, Nicholas McKenzie and all those who wished to remain anonymous. Thank you to Anne Grant who allowed me to use the diary she kept when her own mother was ill. Thank you Irene Merrill for information on Armley and for the wacky telephone calls!

For those who have supplied information for this book—Dick Jackson of the Hull Asbestos Campaign and Iain McKechnie and Harry McLuskey of Clydeside Action on Asbestos, Alan Dalton, Mr T Harkness, John Docherty and Bert Connor—thanks.

A warm thank you to the 'Australian connection'. Many thanks to Ben Hills, author of the Wittenoom story *Blue Murder* who allowed me to freely quote from his book and to the Asbestos Diseases Society of Australia for supplying additional information about Wittenoom. Thanks also to Rolf Harris.

Stories and information used in this book have come from various sources as listed in Appendix 2, but particularly from *Killer Dust*, *Blue Murder*, Steve McQueen and *Victims Twice Over*. Any errors or omissions are purely my own.

Brenda McKessock
January 1995

Contents

Ellen McKessock in the 1950s

1
Ellen's Story

IN APRIL 1992 my mother, Ellen, developed a pain in her back. For the next few months she went through numerous hospital tests as doctors tried to find out what was wrong with her. In December she had a biopsy the result of which was known on Christmas Eve. She had mesothelioma.

The disease got progressively worse throughout 1993. Mum spent most of the summer in hospitals and at the Accord Hospice in Paisley. Eventually she wanted to be home. With her husband Stan, my dad, and I looking after her 24 hours a day, she spent her final months in her own house with her family. She died in her sleep on November 6th 1993, eleven days before her 68th birthday.

This is her story.

Memories of the Past

Ellen Paterson Whitelaw was born on November 17th 1925. She was one of ten children and when her mother died in 1939 she became, at the age of thirteen, a 'little mother' to her younger brothers and sisters.

During the years of the Second World War her father got a job, her brothers went to the forces and Ellen grew into a lovely young lady. She loved music and would often go for a night out to the dancing at the Barrowlands Ballroom in Glasgow. It was here, in 1943, that she met a young sailor from Aberdeen— Stanley McKessock.

On Christmas Day 1946 Ellen and Stan were married. They had six children—Stanley, Thomas, Anne, Ellen, James and Brenda. Ellen and Stan lost all three of their sons. The two eldest boys died young. And tragically in May 1963 two year old James was diagnosed as having leukaemia. In those days there was no cure and no treatment.

A Scottish newspaper picked up the story and ran a series of articles about 'little Jimmy'. Cards, letters and gifts were sent by families from all over Scotland for James. In July his very special third birthday party was gate-crashed by up and coming television stars Bob Monkhouse, Yana and Denis Spicer. James loved it. Less than three months later he was dead.

My parents had to sit and watch my brother die, knowing there was nothing they could do. Thirty years later my dad went through it all again as he watched his wife, whom he had been with for fifty years, die of mesothelioma.

James McKessock's 3rd birthday party in July 1963. James sits on his mother's knee and is surrounded by family, friends and TV stars, Denis Spicer (left), Yana (top) and Bob Monkhouse (right)

Take The Pain Away

In April 1992 mum and I went shopping in Glasgow. We parked the car and walked to the big new St Enoch shopping mall. Mum had a pain in her back which she was determined to ignore. A few years before she had suffered a heart attack so, as usual, we walked slowly. Half an hour later she was breathless and tired so we decided to go home.

"There's something far wrong with me. This isn't right," she said.

At first our local doctor thought that the pain in her back might be a chill or a lung infection. Then he suggested it might be muscular so he gave us a muscle spray. It didn't work. Mum was then sent to various hospitals for tests—X-rays, barium meal, dye in her legs, cameras down her throat. They even tried to take fluid from her lungs—a slightly painful experience. A partial biopsy followed. Still no answers.

In late 1992 I went to see her hospital doctor who assured me that whatever it was that Ellen was suffering from, it was not malignant and they "were keeping a close eye on her".

Slightly rattled, as I'd felt for a while, I knew there was something very wrong. My mother never complained about feeling ill. It wasn't in her character. If she said she felt bad then it had to be serious.

Visiting mum later the same day I discovered that the staff nurse had told her she could use the 'quiet room' if she felt like it. When I arrived she was puzzled and upset.

"What did they mean?" she asked me. "That's for people with things like cancer. So they can cry." No one would tell us what was wrong with her and no one would tell us what they suspected. We were left in a state of knowing something was going on—but what? What did they think? What was it?

More tests followed in December. She visited almost every main hospital in the Glasgow area. On the 19th she went through a biopsy operation and on Christmas Eve the doctors knew what was wrong.

On Boxing Day mum's sister Margaret celebrated her Ruby wedding anniversary. Mum drove her car to the party and back. She enjoyed the party but as the night went on she became afraid that someone might bump into her on the dance floor and hurt her back, so she had only one dance with dad.

Hogmanay was a quiet affair. For the first time that I can ever remember in my life my mum did not get dressed up for the bells. No party frock, no make-up, no perfume, no rushing down the stairs at the last minute fixing her earrings as the new year bells rang out from the television. She couldn't be bothered. After the bells, she went straight to bed.

Early in January 1993 mum and I visited the hospital where we were told about the biopsy result. She had lost 30% lung capacity. She had mesothelioma.

I knew what it was but it was a long time before my parents grasped the full picture. I found out what I could and explained everything to mum as and when she asked. Some people may not want to know the truth—mum did.

By March there appeared to be a lump in her side. The tumour appeared to be in the right lung and it was this side of her body where most of the pain was. We were told it was the nerves which were causing the lump and pain. They were irritated.

In April she went to the supermarket but was too tired, breathless and in pain to do anything but sit down. She never went again.

On 28th April mum went to the Accord Hospice for her very first day visit. (A new wing had been opened in June 1992 by Diana, Princess of Wales and on that day mum's sister Margaret had shaken hands with the Princess). When she returned home mum told us that "they gave me a brandy and put me to bed". She liked it.

Because of her pain, mum had to be treated with kid gloves. Driving to and from hospitals with her was a nightmare. The slightest bump in the road caused her unmentionable pain. She would sit in the front passenger seat surrounded by pillows to cushion her body. I quickly became very aware at just how bumpy and potholed the roads were and, driving reasonably slowly, I also discovered just how impatient some other drivers were. Couldn't they see this old lady in the front surrounded by pillows? Were they blind? Couldn't they think that something might be wrong?

Giving her a hug or a cuddle was another gently-does-it experience. You couldn't actually touch her back with your arms, just pretend to. Unfortunately one member of her family, excited and tearful at seeing her after many years apart, gave her a great big bear hug crushing her in the process. The pain she experienced was excruciating. I had already explained to him how ill she was but I didn't realise that he would try to hug her.

His emotional actions caused her untold suffering for days and after the experience she cried, confused as to why he had hurt her. Naturally he was upset too when he realised what had happened. I could see the look in his eyes which said, "I'm sorry, I didn't mean to."

Over the next few months mum spent long hours on the telephone talking to her relatives, desperately looking for support and comfort. Often she never got it. Some of the family she loved ignored her for a long time. In my mind I tried to understand why. Perhaps they just couldn't cope. They had problems of their own. As for our family, we were strong. I never knew how strong until now. People expected us to break down all the time and we didn't. At least not in public. But the strain was always there, lurking quietly under the surface.

Stress, Frustration & Anger

I remember, sometime in spring 1993, going out for a meal in a restaurant. As I sat at a table I looked over and saw two ladies, about the same age as my mum, sitting chatting at another table. I burst into tears. It was as if I had suddenly realised that my mother would never go out to another restaurant or ever have another bar meal—something she loved doing for a special treat.

Tears are a release, everyone needs to cry. Sometimes I cried but usually in private. Much to my embarrassment and whoever I was with, occasionally I would be completely overwhelmed by grief and sorrow. It didn't matter where I was. Mum cried too but never in front of us. She would tell me sometimes that she "had a wee greet this morning".

The anger was something else though. There was a lot of frustration and pent up, almost violent, anger inside me. On one occasion I was standing in a supermarket check-out queue. Behind me was a couple with a kid who was talking. I became more and more annoyed. Anger built up inside me and it was directed at the kid. I honestly thought I was going to turn round and hit someone—just for the sake of doing it. I wanted to lash out.

The anger was there but it seemed to be at the world in general, not usually at anyone in particular. However, sometimes people get in the way. I would get mad at the people closest to me and once I was the innocent target of someone else's frustration, venom and poison. Thankfully I knew what had caused it.

The anger is still with me and is with many other victims of mesothelioma and their families. It doesn't go away. Perhaps it never will.

The Hospice
For eight weeks mum lived at the Accord Hospice where she received the best care and attention the staff could possibly give her. She enjoyed her first jacuzzi, had her nails painted, her hair done and took part in singsongs in the day room with other patients.

At the hospice they would try various new drugs and combinations of drugs. She suffered from sickness, diarrhoea and the passing of blood. Sometimes she thought she was going to die right there and then.

Dad and I visited her one day and she said, "You

nearly lost me last night. I thought I was dying, I passed a lot of blood . . . everything just came away. I honestly thought I was dying. You nearly lost your wee mammy."

In June a nerve block operation took place where a specialist tried to numb some of the nerves which were causing her pain. The idea was that if it worked another operation could take place to completely kill off the nerves. Then her drugs could be reduced. It didn't work. Instead she developed a very bad rash all over her back, chest and neck and she became ill again.

The Homeopathic Hospital in Glasgow's Great Western Road was where the hospice sent her next for a couple of days. They thought homeopathic medicine and treatment may help her. The couple of days became two weeks as again she responded to new medicine by becoming ill. However she liked the hospital itself. Her bed was beside a large bay window and, aided by a nurse, she could stand and wave cheerio to her visitors.

Mum loved music. It was something which gave her the greatest joy. When she was small she and her brothers and sisters would sing songs around the family piano as their mother played. My grandmother instilled in her children the pleasure of music and the 'wee Whitelaws all grew up with the love of music in their blood.

Mum put me and my sister Ellen through music school. We were taught the accordion and played solo, duets, in groups and with a band in competitions, concerts and tours across Europe and Canada. The band had made a tape in 1981 and my mother always had a copy of it with her.

There were about ten beds in her ward and although she couldn't get out of bed herself, my mum one day decided to brighten things up a bit. Everyone was ill, there was little conversation, everyone was sad. So my mum put her accordion band tape on and turned the volume up. Within a few minutes the other patients were jigging up and down the ward, encouraged by you-know-who.

"I got a row the day," she told me. "I had all the patients dancing up and down the ward. I put your tape on . . . they loved it, they were all dancing. And they're all supposed to be sick! The nurses came running in and chased them all back to bed. It was good fun. I got a row, it was all my fault." And then she laughed!

Although she liked the hospital the treatment didn't really do her any good and soon she was back at the hospice. Her condition deteriorated even more and she could not dress or wash herself without help. Dad and I took turns to visit her, he in the afternoon and me in the evening. This way dad could get a break and I could help her get ready for bed.

It was around this time that she first allowed me to help her wash and for the first time in months I saw her body from the back. I was almost physically sick. She was wasting away. Her legs were painfully thin, bed sores were on her lower back and there were huge red finger marks where she had been scratching at an itch. The worst part was her back passage which was open and sore and there were folds of slack skin around her buttocks where she had lost fat and muscle.

I have a strong stomach but the sight of her body and the thought of what was happening to her made me want to throw up. When helping her wash I had to avert my eyes from her and hold my breath. But I never once allowed her to see any reaction in my face—there was no way she could know what her body looked like and there was no way I'd let her see my reaction. It would have hurt her. Every time I washed her I wanted to break down. But I couldn't. I waited until I got home. And I wanted to kill. I wanted to take out the people who had done this to her.

Sometimes relatives would visit her and I would ask them to stay for maybe an hour. I became very unpopular, particularly if they stayed for two hours and I got mad at them. I didn't mean to get angry, it just happened. They couldn't see what it did to her because they weren't there all the time. Even though she enjoyed the company, it wiped her out and me and dad would be left to pick up the pieces.

Flying High

The cocktail of drugs mum was on would quite often cause her to drift away onto some other planet. Yes, my mother got stoned. She would become slightly detached from reality and was easily confused and heavily influenced by what others told her. I jokingly called her a junkie and in return she would respond by saying, "cheeky wee messin", a sly smile coming to her face as she said it.

And she would sing. Lying on her bed with dad, her sister Margaret or I beside her she would burst into a wee song. Her eyes would glow with joy and her

23

frail voice, always in key, filled the room. When she smiled it was as if the whole room lit up.

The most important drug was morphine and she took this in various forms at various stages of the summer. There was sevredol and MST Continus tablets which are both control-release morphine, diamorph which came with a shunt and needle (which she hated) and oramorph (liquid morphine taken orally). Mum particularly hated the taste of the oramorph and would screw her face up in disgust when she knew she had to take it. She described it as "yeuchy, horrible stuff".

In the hospice two nurses would always give mum her drugs. They both carried log books and every dose and time of dose was systematically recorded. They also had to watch her as she swallowed her morphine, something she couldn't understand. She asked them one day why they were watching her. Did they think she was going to give the drugs to someone else? The nurses joked with her and said she might sell it down the town. "Why would anyone want drugs if they didn't need them?" was her answer.

We used to tease her about being a junkie, being stoned and having a very expensive habit. The nurses would laugh. Most patients' families wouldn't say such a thing, would they? Swallowing doses of oramorph wasn't a pleasant experience but she was amused when I'd say, "there goes another thousand bucks." A slight wry smile would appear. A few minutes later she'd be stoned again.

The dosage of drug was raised every so often as her body became tolerant. In March she had been on

360mg of MST per day. This had upset her when she first went to the hospice and heard two other patients discussing their MST doses. One patient was on 40mg and the other was on 60mg. Mum kept quiet about her dose but it preyed on her mind. In July the dose rose to 1,000mg MST per day plus oramorph if she needed it for in between pain. By August she was on oramorph only and the dose of this by September was 1,800mg per day. By October and November the amount of oramorph she needed daily was well over 2,000mg.

Morphine, an alkaloid of opium, is one of the most powerful narcotic analgesics. In other words it is a controlled drug used, in my mum's case, for the relief of pain in the final stages of her illness. Another analgesic is heroin.

A relative said to me one day, "I hear your mum's on morphine now."

My response was, "she's been on morphine for months." It seemed that once mum went on to liquid morphine, her relatives started to realise just how serious her condition was.

On top of all the morphine mum took other drugs such as antidepressants, antipsychotic drugs, homeopathic medicine, laxatives and antibiotics. I often wondered how long she could go on before the cocktail of drugs, not the tumour, killed her.

Often she would sit and stare into space, unaware of what was going on around her. What was going through her mind? What was she seeing? We'll never know. At other times she was sharp, bright and witty— a glimmer of my real mum.

Her biological clock was disorientated and she would want odd things at odd hours. Time meant very little to her. When she came home to stay dad and I took care of her 24 hours a day. It was a demanding, stressful job. I would do the night shift while dad did the day shift. Her illness made sure we were always busy and often, in the middle of the night, I would have to explain to her that it wasn't dinner time, but it would be breakfast time soon.

On one of those long nights which merged with morning she had me up at 4am. She just wanted company and decided a wee sherry would be nice. With all the drugs she was on, alcohol was not a good idea. But she wanted it, so who was I to deny her? When I returned from the kitchen, sherry in hand, she was asleep. I went to bed. At 4.30am she awoke demanding to know where her sherry was. The pair of us ended up talking well into the early hours of the morning, mum with her sherry and me with a glass of wine.

Home

At first mum said she didn't want to come home. She felt safe in the hospice. She shared a room with two other ladies but, after one of them died, she became distressed. Another lady who then came into the room also died. "Everyone's dying in here," she told me. Mum, feeling sad, felt that she wanted to go home but it was some time before she made the decision.

One day she woke up to find that someone had put a vase of white lilies on her bedside table. To my mother white lilies were associated with death—the flowers in older days that were put on a grave. She was even more upset and I removed them from the room. The hospice staff probably didn't even realise their significance.

The staff nurse, Maria, discussed mum coming home with me and dad. She knew home was the best place for mum but knew that mum was unsure about leaving the safety of the hospice. Soon I discovered the reasons for the reluctance to come home. She was afraid that she would be a burden to her family. Another of her fears was that if she died in the house, dad or I would find her. My mother, in all her pain and agony was more concerned about us than she was about herself! But home was where she wanted to be and home was where she wanted to die. So, in August, home she came.

When we first brought her back from the hospice she slept in her own upstairs bedroom. The distance between her bed and the bathroom was about 20 feet and gradually, as she became more breathless, this was too far for her to walk. I would bathe her but soon just getting in and out of the bath was too much for her, and she became terrified of the bath. So we resorted to sponge down washes or bed baths.

The most distressing part of her illness was the pain. Sometimes, when the effects of her drugs were wearing off, she would cry out. She had set doses of oramorph for set times and in-between smaller doses if such a situation would arise. As her body became tolerant, doses rose. There was a pattern of acceleration. The more she needed, the quicker her body tolerated it. The other side of the coin was that the more drugs she had, the quicker she would die.

She would cry and beg to be helped. "Take the pain away". "Help me, make it stop". When it's someone you love and you're left with their life literally in your hands—in a vicious circle of drugs, pain and death—what do you do? You do your best.

It was around this time when her panic attacks began. Getting to the bathroom was an ordeal and by the time she had walked back to bed she was desperately gasping for air. Thinking her lungs were going to pack up completely she would panic.

The only person who could calm her was me. I would breath with her—big deep breaths as much as possible—and talk to her 'nice and easy' telling her she was doing great and keep going. Eventually, after about 20 minutes, she would relax and her breathing, stilted as it was, would get back to normal. If I wasn't in the room with her she would panic and try to call out for me—thereby using up some of the oxygen she desperately needed.

Getting up and down stairs became too much for her and eventually she was trapped in her room. The hub of activity was in the living room so, no matter how hard we tried, she became isolated.

We decided to make the living room her 'bedsit'. A bed was moved downstairs and part of the settee went upstairs. The district nurse gave us a loan of a chemical toilet and, using the large living room cupboard which had its own window, we created a personal toilet for her.

She liked this new arrangement. She had company and she was comfortable. Knowing she would be confused for the first few nights, I slept on the floor beside her. Once she was settled I returned to my own room.

I had bought a baby intercom and with this I could hear what was going on in the living room. Mum had a bell which she rang if she needed anything. It was very effective, particularly in the middle of the night! Sometimes, for a joke she would ring it "just to see if it's working" or to see "if her servants (me and dad) were listening". She always had a sense of humour!

One day she asked me, "Am I going to die? Am I dying?" At first I was a little stunned. And I felt sad. I knew the answer was Yes. She was lying in bed. I was fixing her covers. She already knew what I might say but it was as if she wasn't sure if I'd tell her the truth— the truth she already knew.

She just had to hear it spoken. Out loud. She just wanted to know. I looked her straight in the eye and quietly said, "Yes mum, you are." She said nothing and I just sat with her for a while as this thought— and who knows what others—went through her mind. I remember thinking, what do you do if your life is at an end? What do you think? What would I think?.

The most frequent person who came to visit was aunty Margaret who came to the house almost every day. Margaret had taken good care of mum all through her illness, visiting her in the hospitals and the hospice and bringing cakes and goodies for wee cups of tea. Margaret washed nighties and clothes and told mum all the latest gossip.

Other relatives, who by now were realising how serious mum's condition was, began visiting more often. But others were still confused as to what was going on. One of them, delighted at the news of mum getting home, told my sister Ellen that it was good that mum was better and out of the hospice.

Ellen replied, "She's not better, she's home to die."

Another relative who had came up from England for a family wedding in September apologised to me for not visiting my mother but that he would "visit her next time". Angry and frustrated I thought, there won't be a next time. There never was.

Looking after someone all day, every day is a very tiring and stressful experience. Sleep patterns are disrupted and sleep itself becomes interrupted and fractured. Responding to mum's bell early in the morning I once fell down the stairs, almost breaking a leg in the process. The reason for my accident was tiredness. Dad, under all the stress, was sometimes irritable usually over minor, unimportant things. On one occasion we ended up screaming at each other over a pot of mince! However the most important person was mum and in the last few weeks of her life dad was the most patient, kindest man in the world to her.

In mid September mum's right eye began to close as the muscle got weaker. She could barely see out of it and the pupil didn't respond to light. Our MacMillan nurse, Innes, would visit once a week and she provided us with a spenco bed (a full length spongy mattress) for underneath mum's sheets. We also got the loan of a sheepskin from the district nurses and this all helped ease mum's painful bed sores.

I had bought her a cushioned ring which she used

for small periods of time when she sat up. Unfortunately a young nurse rather dramatically informed
us, "We don't use them any more. They do more harm
than good". To us the ring helped mum and we only
ever used it for short periods of time. She was dying
and if it relieved some pain for a little while, was it
wrong? Because she had heard the comment mum
became reluctant to use her ring again and had to be
gently coaxed—without it she couldn't sit in a chair
at all.

Final Days
The hardest thing in the world to do is watch someone
you love slowly die. In the last two weeks of my
mother's life I watched her mentally and physically
deteriorate at a rate so alarming no one in our family
could quite believe it. Before our eyes she went from a
fun-loving, strong-willed woman to a baby-like
creature. Finally she was a degenerate zombie. And
we couldn't stop it.

In the summer of 1993 we resolved the question
of 'more painkiller if it's needed'. Mum had decided
herself that if she was in pain, if she needed painkiller,
if it would put her over her dose—even if it killed her
—she wanted it. The decision was hers and hers alone
and, realising that one day she may not be able to
make decisions for herself, she made her wishes clear
to us, her family.

The most important thing was that she shouldn't
suffer. My dad and I strove to make her as happy and
comfortable as possible. We knew she was dying. She
knew she was dying. What was the point of denying

her drugs when she needed them? Especially when, by doing so, we prolonged her agony. By October she had very little quality of life. She didn't want to live, she was just hanging on.

By now the only time she got out of bed was when she went to the bathroom. She needed help for that too. Each day a district nurse would visit and, because of the state of her bed sores, the nurse tried applying comfeel dressings on the bottom of her spine. Disorientated and confused she would pull them off saying, "there's something sticky there."

It was like dealing with a small child. I would patiently explain to her what the sticky things were and that she should keep them on. Eventually she would understand and agree to leave them alone. Five minutes later she'd be back to square one, "but its sticky . . . there's something sticky there" and she'd try to pull them off again. All the understanding had gone.

Mum always kept her sense of humour—right to the end. One day she was sitting in bed with something in her hands. Concentrating deeply, she sat and folded the object which turned out to be my sister's new black velvet hat. I asked her what she was doing.

"Folding."

"What are you folding?"

"Folding, folding."

"What is it?"

"Folding. It's a bag. A wee bag."

"It's not a bag, it's a hat."

"No, it's a bag."

"It's a hat. A velvet hat. It's Ellen's."

"Is it? I'm Ellen."

At this point we showed her that it was a hat and put it on her head. She was delighted with herself.

"Take my picture then." So we did.

She once told me, "If only I had had ten more years. Just ten more years. Then I would have died content." She was staring death in the face and she knew it. Our local doctor was a religious man and sometimes he would say a little private prayer with her. It seemed to calm her.

In her last two weeks of life her condition had deteriorated so badly that thoughts of euthanasia and mercy killing went through my mind. Yes, I'll admit it—I thought it. I wondered about what would happen if I were to put a pillow over her face. Let her out.

Watching her suffer was almost unbearable. I would often sit beside her and think about it. But I felt I didn't have the right. Or maybe I just wasn't strong enough. I don't know but I wondered if people in other families, in the same position as ours, had had the same crazy ideas?

By now mum could no longer walk to her bathroom even although it was only two feet away from the bed. Dad would lift his 'frail wee wifie' up in his arms and carry her there and back.

Swallowing became a problem to her and we had to be very careful not to give her anything that would make her choke. She lost her appetite completely and coaxing her to eat was a long, time-consuming process. I had to time when I thought she'd wake up so that I had something ready for her. Putting it in front of her and spoon feeding her was the only way I could get something into her stomach. A baby cup was bought so she could enjoy a cup of tea without spilling it. Gradually she came off solids completely and went onto liquids—the reverse of what a baby would do. She was going backwards.

Simple things like getting fresh bed sheets gave her the greatest pleasure. It became a knack to change the bed while she went to the bathroom, carried there by dad. I would strip the bed, turn the spenco bed over, get the sheepskin on the bed followed by towels, sheets, pillows and blankets. By the time she was ready to get back in her bed was freshly made for her. Climbing back in she'd coo, "This is lovely. This is great."

The towels under the sheets became necessary when her bed sores got really bad. One sore was huge—at least three inches long and occasionally it would bleed. She couldn't lie in any other way except on her back, so her spine became a pressure point and more sores followed. There was no flesh to separate the bone from the skin so the sores got progressively worse.

On Tuesday 2nd November the doctor paid us a visit. For a few moments he was alone in the room with mum and they said a little prayer. He informed us that her lungs were filling up with fluid and she had "maybe a week left". After he had gone she said to me, "my eyes are full of water . . . fix them tears". Wee soul.

The next day I sat on my knees beside her bed and gently spoon fed her runny custard. She had forgotten how to use a straw (again) so this was re-taught. When she finished her custard she smiled and told me to "tell Bobby that was great". Confused, she was convinced that she had just eaten soup made for her by her brother.

Remember Remember, the Fifth of November

At 2am on the morning of Friday 5th November, I heard mum making a weird noise. Her words would no longer form properly and often she cried out in her sleep. This time she was trying to call out "help"—or was it "hurry" (her two favourite words). It was like trying to communicate with a new baby.

She wanted a drink but was unable to use a straw. Using a syringe I sprayed some water into the side of her mouth. Her mouth, constantly open as she gasped for breath, was always dry and we would spray synthetic saliva (which she thought was wonderful stuff). Calmed, she dozed off to sleep again. For half an hour all was quiet. Then she started calling out again. Attended to by dad she again fell asleep. At 7.30am, we were attending to her again.

At lunchtime my sister Anne helped the two district nurses who came to change the dressings. Mum was almost unconscious and the nurses pulled her this way and that to wash her. She didn't seem to know what was going on and made no noise or response to them.

Her eyes seemed vaguely open but, at this point, I was sure she was almost blind. The stench in the room was unbearable and there was pus on the sheets. We had to open windows even though it was November. The nurses knew that our mother would not be with us for very much longer and, although they were upset themselves, tried to break this gently to us.

We had been offered extra help on several occasions by the district services. A nurse could have been sent to the house to stay with mum overnight so that dad and I could get a proper sleep. Dad turned it down as I knew he would. It wouldn't have made any difference as we would both have lain awake listening for her anyway. Dad refused to sleep anywhere but in the living room with his wife.

Our ears became accustomed to noises. In my room, through the intercom, I would hear what was going on in the living room. I was tuned to the groans, moans and breaths of my mother.

Mum's sore at the bottom of her spine was surrounded by a blue line, evidence that oxygen was not getting to that area of her body. I have never seen or smelled gangrene but I am sure that's what the smell in the living room had been. Not only was oxygen not getting to her spine but I believe it wasn't getting to her brain. All week she had been forgetting things even to the extent that one day she didn't know which of her daughters was with her. She couldn't recognise us.

Some photographs had arrived that morning from mum's goddaughter, Linda in Canada. One of them was a picture, taken in 1979, of mum and Linda at a party. The pair of them were dressed in kilts and tartan bunnets. We passed the photos around and laughed at them. I showed them to mum who smiled weakly. She knew there was a joke and joined in. It was now 3 o'clock in the afternoon. I gave her her painkillers and sat by the bed, talking. I'm sure she didn't even know who was in the room with her. As I held her hand I knew she was completely blind. She fell asleep.

By 8 o'clock that evening she hadn't stirred but we were not too worried as often she would sleep for five or six hours at a time, particularly during the night. At 11pm we became concerned. As I knelt beside her, I held her hand and talked to her.

Her eyes were half open and her chest rose and fell as air went into and out of her lungs. As usual her mouth was open as she desperately gasped for air. From her throat came a strange wailing noise. Was she trying to talk to us? To communicate?

Talking got no response from her. Raising my voice I tried again, stroking her hair at the same time. If she could hear me, I asked, squeeze my hand. No response. Dad, Anne and I decided to call the doctor. What if she was in pain and couldn't tell us?

The doctor arrived and looked at her. Then he turned to us and said, "I think this is her last night. I doubt if she'll wake up". The week before she had told the doctor privately that she was 'at peace' and ready to go. We were not to worry. She would be okay. The noise coming from her throat was being made by her vocal chords. She was in too deep a sleep to know what was going on and could not feel anything.

Dad, as usual, was sleeping in the living room. Just after midnight (now the early hours of Saturday 6th November) Anne and I went upstairs to bed. Before I left I held mum's hand and, stroking her hair, I said, "Poor wee mammie." Lying in bed I was half dozing but I couldn't quite get to sleep. In the living room dad was making up his bed. He switched the television off.

Silence. Something was missing. Then dads' voice. "Brenda, Anne."

Mum had gone.

Afterwards

In the early hours of the morning we called the funeral directors and made arrangements for mum's cremation. Dad, Anne and I were calm and controlled throughout which must have thrown people slightly. At 9am we started calling close relatives with the news. This was the hardest thing in the world. Over the telephone sisters, brothers and close family of mum's burst into tears. I became upset at their grief, not my own.

A doctor at the funeral parlour informed us that as mum died of mesothelioma a postmortem may be required—particularly if we had a court case pending. This was news to us. The procurator fiscal became involved and the powers-that-be decided we had enough evidence from earlier biopsies so no post-mortem was required. Mum's cremation took place five days later once everything had been sorted out.

On the morning of the funeral I went privately to see my mother. She lay in her coffin covered by a white gown-like shroud. Her face was pale. Her eyes and mouth were closed. The mouth had an unnatural pose and I wondered how many bones they'd broken. There was white make-up on her eyelids. She looked so small. But this tiny frail body was not my mother—this was a shell. Mum had long since gone.

The service was as mum had wanted it. It was lovely and I knew it was exactly as she would wished. At the end some music she had specifically requested—*Intermezzo* from *Cavaliera Rusticanno*—was played. Our family were still calm but at the service everyone, except Ellen and dad, broke down. Ellen had been running around waving a bottle of valium at everyone all morning! For me, it was when I saw them bring in the coffin that did it. This was really the end. I broke down. It was a few minutes before I brought myself back under control.

I often wondered why we were so calm throughout everything. Sometimes I would see people looking at us as if they were expecting some emotion. The truth is we had mourned backwards. All through the months of mum's illness we had grieved. At the time of her death there was an overwhelming sense of relief. She was out of pain. The weight—the agony, the stress, the watching her suffer—had been lifted.

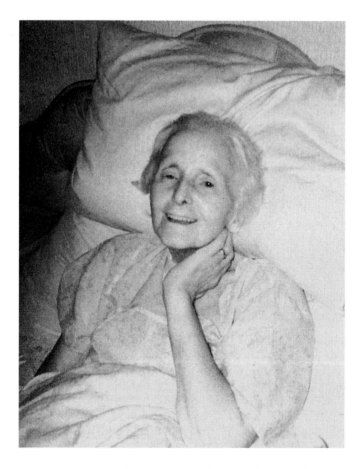

Ellen McKessock in October 1993, 12 days before she died

2

Asbestos

— Out of the Soil

WHEN I BEGAN to learn more about mesothelioma, I started to wonder what exactly had gone on in my mother's body. I knew the tumour was in the pleura of her lungs but what about the secondary cancers that mesothelioma threw out?

Her right eye had started to close in September. At the time a friend of my sister who was an opthalmic optician had mentioned that once he had seen a patient who had a tumour on the brain. The eye started to close. Had mesothelioma caused this in my mother? Later when I sorted out her affairs I discovered that she had been making mistakes in her bank book as far back as 1992. It was as if she couldn't add 2 to 12—very simple arithmetic. This was puzzling as she'd always been very accurate. Why had she forgotten how to count ?

In 1984 my mother had suffered a heart attack. At the time we were stunned. She always seemed healthy—she was one of those people who never smoked a cigarette in her life, enjoyed fruit, vegetables, all-bran, all the things that are good for you, and avoided cakes and fatty things. She kept herself active by going swimming and dancing. Occasionally she had a glass of sherry or brandy.

Another heart attack followed in 1988. There seemed no logical reason at that time either. She didn't smoke or drink, she took regular exercise and she was careful with her diet. She did everything right and yet she was the one with the heart condition.

The secondary cancers caused by mesothelioma attack other organs—the liver, the heart. Had my mum's heart attacks been caused by mesothelioma? It made me wonder what would have happened if she had died in 1984 or 1988. Her death certificate would have read 'heart disease'. We would never have known about the mesothelioma. (Her death certificate does, in fact, state heart disease as a secondary cause).

How many others had died with asbestos related diseases lurking unknown in their bodies? How many had 'heart disease' on their death certificate?

"Thousands," John Docherty (formerly of Clydeside Action on Asbestos) told me. After all, a 1993 report showed that 40% of death certificates do not state the correct cause of death.

In April 1994 Glasgow was named as the 'heart disease capital of the world' in a report by the World Health Organisation. Cigarette smoking and high cholesterol levels were blamed. The report showed that women in the north of Glasgow had the highest heart disease rate in the world in the 1980s and men had the second highest death rate, second only to an area in Finland.

Asbestos is a naturally occurring mineral, deposits of which have been found throughout the world. There are two groups—chrysolite and amphiboles.

Chrysolite, white asbestos, comes from serpentine rock and its fibres are soft and curly.

There are five types of amphiboles—amosite, anthophyllite, crocidolite, tremolite and actinolite (brown/grey, white, blue, white and white respectively) and their fibres are small and straight.

Asbestos fibres are in fact, so small that two million of them could fit onto a pin head. To the naked eye they are invisible.

Asbestos has been mined all over the world, in every continent. The white asbestos, chrysolite, is the most abundant of the types and has been found in large quantities in Canada. Blue asbestos, crocidolite, has been found only in South Africa and Australia and has been proven to be at least sixty times more dangerous than white asbestos. However all types of asbestos are known to cause cancer.

Used by humans for thousands of years, the mineral was named asbestos by the ancient Greeks who, after discovering it on Cyprus, found it to be incredibly resistant. It could not be destroyed. Asbestos was their word for 'inextinguishable'. From four thousand years ago ancient bowls made of clay and asbestos have been discovered in Finland.

In the twentieth century the mining of asbestos became big business. Large international companies pulled it out of the ground and exported it around the globe, both in its raw state and in asbestos products. Asbestos became one of the most important finds of the century and was hailed as the 'magic mineral'. It could be used for almost everything.

After processing, the original colouring of white, blue and brown asbestos changes and they all look similar to the naked eye. Only laboratory tests can distinguish between them. Traces of blue asbestos (the most lethal to humans) can be found amongst white and brown thereby making all asbestos dangerous if it is breathed in by the unsuspecting.

Resistant to heat and corrosion, asbestos fibres are strong and flexible. It was used throughout the industrial world in thousands of common everyday products such as (are you ready for this?) building and insulation materials, cement, pipes, fire resistant coatings on ships, structural girders, car brake linings and clutch plates, rubber, plastic, rope, boiler and pipe packing, pipe coverings, insulation blocks and board, insulation jackets, spray on structural heat insulation, electrical insulation tape, transformers, condensers, cables, conduits, electrical wire insulation, spark plugs, switch boxes, circuit breakers, gaskets, bearing packings, seals, conveyor belting, wall sheets, gas pipes, water pipes, sewage pipes, reinforced asphalt, vinyl floor tiles, linoleum, panels, partitions, clapboard, asphalt siding and shingles, putties, ceiling boards, millboard, stucco, plaster, artificial wood, sound proofing, acoustic tile facings, paint, caulking, asbestos felt, cloth, sheets, blankets, curtains (including fire curtains in theatres), ribbon, artificial snow, filler in rubber goods, welding electrodes, cigarette filters, gas mask filters, filter cloths, filter pads, filter paper, catalyst supports for sulphuric acid production, water proof bearing and packings, cardboard, paper boat hulls, aeroplane wings, lamp wicks and burners, prison cell padding, fire hoses, mail bags, motion picture screens, frying pan handles, rocket re-entry nosecones, piano padding, military helmet lining, cartridges, car undercoating, fire proof safety clothing, life jackets, moulds, pottery and sculpture clay, ironing boards, pot holders, table pads, oven gloves and children's play dough.

Another use of asbestos was in the cigarette sweets which were popular with many children who played at smoking (just like the grownups) and the lacing of talcum powder. Used by women across the world for their own personal hygiene, lethal talc was applied to personal areas of the body and very generously applied to babies bottoms. Condoms, dusted with talc, have also been found to contain asbestos. (In the early 1990s several cases of genital and ovarian cancer amongst women in the UK were blamed on talcum powder which had contained asbestos.) Asbestos can even be used in the filters of beer, fruit juice and medicine and in the early 1940s was used in the filters of gas masks. It is found in ships, shipyards, hospitals, schools and houses in roofs, walls and floors.

Smoking is now known to be a major cause of

lung cancer and asbestos was used in the filter tips of cigarettes and, being a good binding material, was used in the actual paper which covered the tobacco.

In the 1960s, when the threat asbestos posed to human health became blatantly clear, and governments could no longer ignore it, its use became diminished. The highly dangerous blue asbestos was banned in the UK in 1971. By this time however, asbestos was firmly established around the world and its fibres were in the atmosphere. In his book *Blue Murder*, Ben Hills describes how invisible asbestos fibres are now a part of our global ecosystem. They are in the air streams of Siberia and have been found in middle eastern desert sands.

For many decades the main producer of asbestos has been Russia (the former Soviet Union). When the Berlin wall came down the western world got its first real glimpse of the very heavily industrialised eastern block countries. The view was horrific. Pollution, toxic waste and radiation leaks were common. Even today Russia still produces more asbestos than any other country in the world. Conditions in these asbestos mines and factories are, more than likely, a lot worse than in their western counterparts.

For centuries there have been health problems associated with asbestos. Over two thousand years ago Roman slaves became sick while weaving asbestos fibres. Their masters gave them face masks made from animal bladder skins to help protect them from the lethal dust.

By the end of the 1800s the whole process of industrialisation meant that asbestos was being mined and transported across the world to be processed for widespread use. In Manchester and Birmingham factories sprang up where workers, mainly women, spun and weaved asbestos fibres. Health problems appeared amongst the women, most of whom were still in their 30s. They developed chesty coughs, then they sickened and then they died. In 1898 the Lady Inspector of Factories wrote that workers amongst asbestos had more injuries (sickness) than any other workers she was aware of.

In 1906 a British government investigation brought to light the true killing nature of asbestos. The first death ever to be scientifically proven to be caused by asbestos exposure was that of a young man of 33. He had been the last survivor of ten men who had worked in a dust covered room at an asbestos textile plant. The autopsy showed conclusively that he was killed by asbestos. There was no doubt. Twenty-one years later the disease was named—asbestosis.

A study of asbestosis was done in England in 1930 by Merewether, a doctor from the Home Office, and Price, a ventilation engineer. They examined 363 men and women who had been working with and around asbestos. Of these, 127 had asbestosis and the study concluded that only six months' exposure to asbestos was enough to cause the disease and that, after twenty years' exposure, most of these asbestos workers could be expected to have developed the illness.

Even after reports such as these, nothing was done to protect workers around Britain and Europe from the effects of asbestos exposure. In 1939 World War II broke out and asbestos related products were very much in demand for the war effort. The war in Europe ended in 1945 and by 1946 there had been 235 asbestos related deaths in Britain.

Asbestosis was not the only disease caused by asbestos exposure. By the 1930s lung cancer, cancer of the bowel, cancer of the stomach and cancer of the oesophagus had all been linked to asbestos.

Mesothelioma, a tumour of the lining of the lung or abdomen, was once a medical condition so rare some doctors doubted its very existence. By the 1960s mesothelioma was losing its rarity status as more people around the world developed the disease after being exposed to blue asbestos.

The Diseases of Asbestos

Asbestosis
Asbestosis is a type of scarring (fibrosis) of the lungs. It is caused by asbestos fibres which have been inhaled into the lungs by the victim. Exposure to asbestos has usually occurred over several years and most people, mainly men, have worked closely with asbestos in shipyards or factories.

The latent period (the time it takes to develop asbestosis from the time of exposure) is about 15 – 30 years. One sufferer described asbestosis as feeling as if his lungs were gradually filling up with wet concrete. The lungs lose their elasticity making breathing increasingly difficult. Pains in the chest are common and sufferers often have a rattly cough.

The lungs can become distorted due to the scar tissue and adhesions may develop in the lung, the diaphragm and in the outer lining of the heart.

There is no cure.

Pleural Thickening & Pleural Plaques

Asbestos fibres sometimes work their way out of the lung through to its lining—the pleura. Pleural plaques can occur here and in the lining of the chest wall. Plaques usually develop before fibrosis although the plaques themselves do not become malignant.

Pleural thickening occurs when the asbestos fibres cause a thickening of a large pleural area. The victim becomes breathless as lung movement is restricted by the disease.

Pleural plaques are similar to pleural thickening but appear in small individual areas rather than one large one. Again, pain and breathing problems are usual.

There is no cure.

Lung Cancer

Lung cancer is normally associated with cigarette smoking but it can also be caused by asbestos exposure. The latency period is about 20 years and, if caught in time, lung replacements have occasionally enabled a victim to recover.

Asbestos and smoking have a multiplicative effect on lung cancer development. Smokers amongst asbestos workers are 8 times more at risk of getting lung cancer than smokers who do not work with asbestos.

Cancers & Carcinomas

A carcinogen is any substance which produces cancer. Carcinomas of the larynx, abdomen (including the intestine, peritoneum, oesophagus and stomach) and bowel have been linked to asbestos exposure.

Cases of cancers of the ovary, hoemopoitic (blood forming) system, breast and mesothelioma in the lining of the testes have appeared but as yet, they have not been scientifically confirmed.

Mesothelioma

Possibly the most horrific of all the asbestos related diseases, mesothelioma is a tumour which grows inside the lining of the lung or the lining of the abdomen (mesothelioma can also occur in the lining of the testes). With pleural mesothelioma the sufferer experiences increasing breathlessness and pains in the back and chest. The latency period is the longest and can be anything from 10 to 60 years. Once diagnosed the victim has usually only months to live.

There is no cure.

Emphysema, Chronic Bronchitis & Chronic Obstruction of the Airways

Emphysema is a disease which causes the destruction of the alveoli walls. Alveoli are small sacs in the lungs which control the flow of air and blood. The partially destroyed lungs lose the power to work properly and the sufferer finds breathing difficult.

Chronic bronchitis is a disease where the victim's air passages become inflamed. It can be caused by smoking, the inhalation of dust or pollution and viral infections. Sufferers usually have a cough and mucus builds up.

Chronic obstruction of the airways, COAD, is a rather vague disease. It is similar to emphysema and chronic bronchitis. There is an obstruction in the airflow.

Normally attributed to smoking, recent research has uncovered evidence that emphysema, chronic bronchitis and chronic obstruction of the airways can be caused by exposure to dust and coal. In many cases the sufferer has never smoked.

These diseases are caused by exposure to dust (not necessarily asbestos). They do not 'run in the family' as sometimes is commonly believed.

3
Mesothelioma

THERE ARE TWO main types of mesothelioma: pleural mesothelioma which occurs in the lining of the lungs; and peritoneum mesothelioma which occurs in the lining of the abdomen. Mesothelioma is a rare disease and of the two types, peritoneum mesothelioma is the rarest.

Pleural Mesothelioma

Inside the chest are two lungs, the right and left lung. The lungs are protected by the rib cage and in between the ribs are muscles. These rib muscles, along with the diaphragm, are essential for breathing. The part of the brain which controls breathing receives signals from the body about how much oxygen is required. In turn the brain sends messages along nerves to the muscles, allowing the correct amount of air to be breathed.

Lungs are an incredible breathing machine. Inside each lung is a mass of fine tubes and the lung itself is like a sponge. The smallest of the fine tubes have ends which are called alveoli. These alveoli are actually tiny air sacs and there are about 300 million of them.

On the outside of the lung is the pleura which is a lining tissue. It lies between the lung and the chest wall and it wraps itself around the lung. It has two layers (membranes) and, in between these two layers is the pleural cavity. Inside the pleural cavity is a small amount of fluid. As we breath the two layers of the pleura slide back and forth over each other allowing the lung to contract and expand.

Mesothelioma is a tumour which grows inside the pleural cavity, hindering the movement of the lungs and causing increasing breathlessness in the victim.

The first symptoms of the tumour are usually breathlessness, chest pain and tiredness. The pleural cavity may start to fill up with fluid and cough or fever can develop.

As the tumour grows it fills the pleural cavity. Lung movements become restricted. Eventually the tumour may fill most or all of the pleural cavity. The victim cannot breath properly and the heart must work harder to pump what oxygen there is around the body.

As the tumour grows the pleura gets thicker. A normal pleura is about as thick as a cigarette paper but when mesothelioma takes hold the tumour can grow to several inches in thickness and totally enclose the lung. Under this pressure the lung collapses.

Pleural tumours have been recorded for the last two hundred years but there has been debate about whether they are the same as or different from normal lung cancer. Only in the last twenty years have they been regarded as a separate disease.

Peritoneum Mesothelioma

Peritoneum mesothelioma is very similar to pleural mesothelioma except it develops in the lining of the abdomen. The victim's stomach area swells over a period of time.

Most cases of mesothelioma are caused by direct or indirect exposure to asbestos dust or fibres. Exposure to high levels of asbestos in a short period of time or exposure to low levels of asbestos over a long period of time can induce mesothelioma. What triggers the disease is the amount of asbestos fibres which are left in the lung after exposure.

There is a long delay between asbestos exposure and obvious signs of the tumour but it lies somewhere between ten and sixty five years. In most cases the period is thirty to forty years.

Exposure does not have to take place over a long period of time—just one small instant could be enough. If the asbestos fibres lodge themselves in the victim's body, chances of mesothelioma development are relatively high. Smoking can cause lung cancer and it too can have a major impact on mesothelioma development.

Because it is so rare mesothelioma has no cure. Treatments such as chemotherapy, radiotherapy and even surgery have usually been ineffective with only a small number of people gaining any (short term) benefit. In the area around the lungs nerves can become irritated causing increasing pain for the sufferer.

Acupuncture and nerve block operations have been tried on patients in the past, the idea of these is to freeze or kill off irritated nerves in order to relieve some of the pain. Homeopathy, aromatherapy and reflexology have also been attempted. However pain control, through drugs, is usually the only thing that can be done.

Used mainly for insulation purposes, processed asbestos was used for many years in the shipbuilding and industrial sectors, exposing many people (mainly men) to unknown health problems in their later years. Over the last two decades cases of mesothelioma—which is known to have been the direct cause of deaths of 6% of asbestos workers—have dramatically increased as people who were exposed to asbestos during the 1940s, 1950s, 1960s and 1970s develop the disease.

There is no research on mesothelioma going on anywhere in the world in medical universities, the reason being that it has been considered so rare.

Mesothelioma is malignant (depending on what you read) and is not malignant (depending on what else you read). Some doctors will often refer to mesothelioma as cancerous, some other doctors will view it as non-cancerous. Needless to say, even in the medical world, there are many different opinions about this disease and what seems to be a great deal of ignorance.

The length of time a victim may have left to live once mesothelioma has been diagnosed is also hard to pin down. The average time span from mesothelioma being diagnosed through to death is thought to be about seven months.

The initial cause of the disease, asbestos fibres, lie silently dormant in the victim's body for decades and it is now widely believed that biopsies speed up the rate of growth of the tumour. Without a biopsy some people have lived for over three years.

Ignorance about asbestos and mesothelioma is rife, even those in the medical profession know very little—or will admit to knowing only very little. The general public know even less. In 1992 an acquaintance of our family who had just been told he had mesothelioma turned to his wife and said, "It's not as bad as I thought. It's not cancer." By 1993 he was dead. Mesothelioma was once described to me by a doctor, as "a vicious and particularly nasty tumour".

In the autumn of 1993 a British television company broadcast a documentary about the town of Armley in England which had been covered in asbestos dust. The dust had come from a local factory which had long since been shut down. The unfortunate residents of the town were warned not to disturb the dust in any way.

Many people in the town had died or were dying from mesothelioma and asbestosis. A couple of 'asbestos experts' had gone to the town to talk to the townspeople, many of whom were complaining that they couldn't sell their homes because of the dust. In one house where the attic had been converted into an extra room, a young couple eagerly showed their home to the experts. They explained how, after pulling down plasterboard in the attic, they had discovered blue asbestos in a corner. This was their baby's room.

The official line is that asbestos is safe as long as it is kept in good order and always covered in paint or something similar. Some would ask, "Is it worth the risk?"

Asbestos is a very dangerous substance—ask those who are suffering because of it—and the deeper you dig into the subject, the more facts you uncover, the more aware you become of the big 'cover-up' that has gone on throughout the industrial world.

Aliens is a 1989 Twentieth Century Fox block-buster action-packed horror film. The alien was a creature with acid for blood which gestates inside the body. Mesothelioma is worse than any Alien movie. It is no figment of the imagination. It is real. Who would want something resembling a horse's saddle inside their chest ? Because that's what mesothelioma is.

It is a time bomb. It waits patiently inside its victim's body for decades until one day it starts to strangle their lungs. As it progresses it attacks other organs such as the liver and heart by throwing out secondary cancers. Sometimes the heart is damaged first, years before the lethal strangulation of the lungs begins.

"The actual tumour which mesothelioma prod-uces is worse than anything any horror film could imagine," says Iain McKechnie of the pressure group Clydeside Action on Asbestos. "It is hideous." The tumour is thick and hard. It's as if it is made of really tough leather. It is hard and horny—extremely tough. You could chisel it with a sharp instrument."

A leading pathologist once said, "Once you see mesothelioma you NEVER forget it." Mesothelioma is a slow silent painful killer. No-one deserves it. Asbestos is the only known cause.

Or is it?

Karain (English translation, 'Pain In The Belly') is a small village in Turkey which had, in the 70s, a population of 600-800 people. Between 1970 and 1974, an epidemic of mesothelioma broke out causing the deaths of twenty four villagers. The puzzling thing was that there was no asbestos to be found in the area. A 1978 study of the village threw up the possibility that volcanic activity was causing the problem. Zeolites, volcanic silicates, have fibres which are very similar to asbestos fibres.

In the western world replacements for asbestos have been produced since the 1930s. One of these is glass fibre. Again glass fibre has a very similar fibre structure to asbestos. In the 1960s 'fibre glass pneumoconiosis' (fibre glass lung scarring) was causing asthma, pneumonia, bronchitis, chest pain, breathing and nose problems, sore throats and coughing in humans.

In 1976 a family of four installed a central heating system in their home. The mother, father and their two children (aged eleven and eight) began to suffer from chest and breathing problems. Their dog had so much difficulty breathing he had to be humanely put to sleep. The dog had cancer which had spread to the lungs and, inside the lungs, were glass fibres. The air-duct lining of the central heating system was made of glass fibre.

In trying to produce an asbestos substitute, scientists had recreated fibres which were similar in length and width to asbestos itself and could still cause serious damage to health.

4

Towns of Tragedy

Old Town, Hebden Bridge

The year is 1974 and the people of Wodsworth, otherwise known as Old Town Hebden Bridge, are concerned about the growing number of asbestos related deaths in the area.

Acre Mill, which stands at the top of the hill above the town, was once an asbestos factory and in this small Yorkshire village many of the residents worked there. So far over 150 of them are dead or dying from asbestosis or mesothelioma. That number would continue to rise in the future.

In production for over thirty years the asbestos factory, owned by Cape Asbestos, was eventually closed in 1971. The people who worked there were never told of the dangers of asbestos and mothers and fathers took the deadly dust, stuck to their clothes, unknowingly home to their children. Women ate their lunch amongst the fibres, they played games with raw asbestos making make-believe wigs and carrying on 'for a laugh'.

Cape Asbestos Ltd, now Cape Industries, was the second largest multinational asbestos company in the UK. At Acre Mill raw asbestos was made into asbestos textile products.

In all the time the factory was open the Factory Inspectorate never once prosecuted Cape Asbestos, even although conditions at the factory were found to be in violation of the British government's 1931 Asbestos Regulations. The Inspectorate, who theoretically should have been protecting the health of the workers in the factory, never seemed to have ensured that Cape Asbestos handled asbestos in a safe way.

Brian Schnacke, an ex-employee, recalled how the extractors rarely worked because they were blocked and he and fellow workers often stood in blue dust a foot deep.

By 1974 Cape Asbestos had paid out an estimated £400,000 to victims, no cases of whom ever went to court. By 1979 the cost had risen to £2 million. The mill was taken over by Raedalen Ltd, a synthetic fibre processor and manufacturer. The Factory Inspectorate insisted that the mill was clean (they cleaned it three times) and that there was absolutely no danger from asbestos.

In the next few years a Hebden Bridge Asbestos Group sprang up. Public meetings were called and the Old Town residents demanded to know what had been going on at Acre Mill. They wanted an inquiry.

More cases of asbestosis and mesothelioma appeared. There were 77 known deaths by 1979—57% of these were caused by lung cancer or mesothelioma, 24% by heart failure, 14% by pneumonia and 5% by asbestosis. Asbestos claimed the lives of six people in one family. A man who worked at the mill for only nine weeks when he was aged thirty five developed lung disease and died of mesothelioma at the age of forty eight.

A government enquiry was set up and Cape Asbestos spent £500,000 on an advertising campaign to convince people that asbestos was safe.

The townspeople were also concerned about where asbestos had been dumped. Where was it? Was it dangerous? In response to this Cape Industries (as they were now known) sent their own team of investigators to dumping grounds and ensured the public that there was absolutely nothing to worry about—no asbestos, everything's fine, it's all perfectly safe.

Some asbestos products had been found at Midgley and Carr Head, Pecket Well but, the public were assured, these were not dangerous and were well covered.

A theatrical play about the Hebden Bridge Massacre (as it was now called) was performed in the town in August 1978 by a northern theatrical group. The play was based on one of the mill's ex-employees, Arthur Montgomery, who died of asbestosis the same month. The theatre group were subsequently sacked.

In 1980 part of the now half demolished Acre Mill

was transformed into a classic car museum. The massacre at Acre Mill was almost forgotten. By this time however, 262 ex-mill workers out of a total of approx 2,200 people had an asbestos related disease. (Many ex-workers have never been traced because, after the war, immigrants to the UK were employed there).

In 1982 ITV screened a television documentary *Alice, a fight for life* which focused on Alice Jefferson, a woman fighting for her life against mesothelioma. The tragedy of Acre Mill was once again in the spotlight. By now over 100 former employees (or their relatives) had died and another 300 had been diagnosed as having an asbestos related disease.

Plans were drawn up to have Acre Mill demolished and the site around it cleared. Suggestions of a car park for the museum and a children's play area were put forward and the local council were not amused when a member of the Asbestos Group claimed to have found asbestos (which was later analysed and found to be asbestos) in the area. The group were accused of hindering the clean up operation. The site was eventually landscaped and grassed over.

A member of staff at the Halifax Environmental Health office told me (in February 1994) that the site of the old mill was now a park. "Perfectly safe, it's all clean," he said. (He became rather agitated at my questions). When I went to the local post office at Wodsworth I wondered if the people there remembered the old mill or were even aware of its very existence. The impression I had was that it had been forgotten. How many children now played on the 'park'?

The Scout Road Tip was one of Cape Asbestos's dumping grounds and in 1993, the West Yorkshire Management Authority discovered asbestos on the surface of the soil. Public pathways had been closed off. Animal burrowing and landslips had brought previously covered asbestos waste up to the surface. Asbestos doesn't go away. If it isn't buried deep enough, the elements and animals eventually bring it back to the surface.

By the end of the 1980s the asbestos related death toll in the Old Town of Hebden Bridge was over 200. The number will increase. Now, in the 1990s there is another town, not very far from Hebden Bridge, where the grim asbestos reaper has yet again raised his ugly head.

Armley

In 1993 the town of Armley near Leeds appeared on the pages of British newspapers. The reason? It was a town with an unusual epidemic. Mesothelioma had claimed the lives of at least 180 of the townspeople. An old asbestos factory which had closed in 1958 had spread the lethal asbestos dust around the town exposing men, women and children.

The factory, JW Roberts was taken over in 1921 by one of the largest asbestos producers in the world— Turner & Newall (now T&N). Asbestos 'snow drifts' were a common sight in the streets as the factory bellowed its poison from chimneys. Inside the building workers were covered from head to toe in white dust. Outside, kids played in the stuff.

Children sitting on their father's knee in the

evening were exposed to the asbestos dust which was all over his work overalls. Women washed dirty dusty clothes belonging to members of their family, men and women who worked in the factory. Outside homes, dust gathered on window ledges and rooftops. Inside it became ingrained on carpets and furnishings. Residents of Armley recall how factory employees came home with their coats and clothes covered in asbestos. Walking through their house they would leave behind a trail of asbestos dust, fibres and 'fluff'.

Irene Merrill, a member of the local campaign for an asbestos-free Armley told me, "I've got asbestos in the door hinges and in the windows of my house. I don't clean in the crevices because I might disturb it". Asked why she still lives there she said, "This is my home. I've got roots here and family."

When the campaign began against T&N many locals, particularly of the older generation were horrified that their town would be dragged into the media and get unwanted, bad publicity.

Irene said, "At first some of the older folk were annoyed at us for kicking up a fuss about asbestos. They thought we were just causing trouble. But I think now they're beginning to realise that we're not just fighting for us, we're fighting for our kids. So now they support us just that little bit more."

T&N denied all responsibility saying they were not aware that the deaths in the town from meso-thelioma were linked to their factory. Evidence uncovered in 1993 proves that they lied.

Residents of the town, where new cases of mesothelioma will no doubt emerge over the next few years, cannot sell their homes because of the asbestos. They are trapped in the mortgage and money pit. As many of the houses are now owner-occupied, the local council expects the residents to pick up the bill for decontaminating the area. T&N, when asked by local campaigners to help, replied in a letter dated 5th November 1993:

"The Armley factory to which you refer was owned and operated by JW Roberts Limited. That company was, and still is, a wholly-owned subsidiary of T&N plc. That fact alone does not give rise to any legal liability on this company's part."

JW Roberts Ltd of Leeds

JW Roberts Ltd began as a family business in 1870, set up by John William Roberts who died in 1896. The company produced low-pressure steam gland and water pump packings and asbestos was introduced sometime before the turn of the century. John's wife and three sons, Clifford, Norman and John, continued the family business into the new century. When the company was amalgamated with Turner & Newall Ltd, Clifford Roberts joined the original board of directors of the 'new' company.

One of the uses of asbestos at the factory was as insulation for the boilers of steam locomotives. Sacks of crude asbestos would be laid over these massive boilers, which were several feet high and long, and there was often a lot of spilling of the crude asbestos as the sacks were removed later. By 1906 even the very sacks themselves were made of asbestos cloth.

(Remember the first death scientifically proven to have been caused by asbestos was in 1906.)

Turner & Newall were attracted to JW Roberts because of the latter's close relationship with the Washington Chemical Company. Unlike other manufacturers who used white asbestos, Washington Chemical used raw blue asbestos, supplied by Roberts, in their Magnesia Plastic product.

JW Roberts were producing blue asbestos textiles, packings, jointings and insulating mattresses for locomotive boilers by 1918. In Kimberley, South Africa were diamond mines and it was in this area that blue asbestos was mined and shipped to Yorkshire.

By 1927 the Armley factory was also producing blue asbestos yarns, corrugated asbestos paper and asbestos felts. In 1930 the asbestos spraying process was introduced and the Roberts factory supplied sprayed asbestos coatings for insulation to the British and other navies, merchant ships, oil tankers, buildings and railway carriages throughout the world.

So successful was the sale of products from Armley that, in the 1950s, Turner & Newall—now called Turner Brothers Asbestos Co Ltd—built a new factory at Hindley Green. This factory was to produce mattresses, spray fibre and blue asbestos textiles.

In 1958 the Armley factory was closed. The new owners were TAC Construction Materials Ltd of Manchester—a large firm which had links to asbestos and other materials. Under the name Hindustan Ferodo, Turner & Newall opened a new factory in Ghatkopar, Bombay in India. The factory is still there and pollution from asbestos dust is still going on to this very day.

Half a tonne of blue asbestos was discovered at four Armley factories in February 1978. TAC (formerly TAC Construction Materials Ltd) spent approx £12,000 decontaminating the sites which they said was done from a moral—not legal—obligation. Fifteen years later concrete, which had been poured over dumped asbestos at the back of one of the factories, began to crack and blue asbestos fibres were found inside the 'clean' factory. It was claimed that the original clean up operation had been nothing more than a public relations exercise.

In the 1980s a spate of asbestos related deaths drew the attention of the local media particularly as some of the victims had not actually worked in the factory. They had just been local townspeople.

One victim, Margaret Ibbetson, had worked in a local Co-op which was near the Armley factory. She had never been in direct contact with asbestos but died of mesothelioma at the age of sixty. Another victim, a sixty four year old woman, told how the local school was 100 yards away from the factory. She described how asbestos had covered the playground. Children skipped and played in it. Seventy-seven year old Agnes Whelan died of mesothelioma—her home was half a mile away from the factory.

The end of the 1980s brought to public attention more death and illness caused by asbestos exposure. Armley was a contaminated town and, even thirty years after the Roberts' factory had closed, the death toll was still rising. And it would continue to rise.

Armley was another Hebden Bridge and, like there, the residents set up their own group—the Armley Asbestos Campaign—and demanded an inquiry. This was in 1992. In the previous sixteen years mesothelioma had claimed the lives of 180 people. One year later the go-ahead for an enquiry was given by Leeds City Council, who claimed to have known nothing of the town's contamination until 1988. The council were accused of a cover-up. Council documents dating from the late 1970s had mysteriously been destroyed.

And still people died. Mesothelioma killed Gladys Keddie, a seventy eight year old who had worked in the Armley factory between 1940–1942. Asbestos dust and fibres were clearly in the air inside the building and, because conditions were so bad, Gladys used to eat her lunch under the stairs.

A meeting of councillors in July 1992 discussed the Armley asbestos pollution problem and John Battle (MP for Leeds West) stated that each house could be cleaned at a cost of £7,500. The total cost is over £6 million.

One of the trusts of the Thatcher governments in the 1980s was the encouragement of more people in the UK to own their own home. Publicly owned council houses across the country were bought by sitting tenants. In Armley the house buying pattern was not much different from any other town.

Of the contaminated houses in Armley, 66% are owner-occupied. The council is reluctant to pay for the cleansing operation and only a means-tested grant is available to home owners (only 20% of whom would qualify for a full grant).

The end of 1992 saw renovation work being banned in Armley. Residents were warned not to clean their lofts and the local property market slumped. Houses were unsaleable. T&N refused to make any contribution towards decontamination.

Chase Manhattan are a multinational company. In 1993 they began proceedings to sue T&N for the asbestos contamination of their main office block in New York. The block was completed in 1961 and contains about 560 tonnes of sprayed limpet asbestos—this coating is now deteriorating.

$185 million is the amount Chase wants from T&N. Unlike British lawyers, who were denied access to T&N's documents, American lawyers were given access. In a warehouse in England millions of T&N papers were seized and shipped back to the USA. A rather telling memo (written by a T&N public relations officer) stated,

"I hope very much that we are never called upon to discuss Armley in the public arena."

Although other office blocks have been contaminated with the sprayed asbestos, Chase Manhattan are the first company to sue T&N. Their claim is that T&N knew asbestos was dangerous but kept that fact quiet. Other companies have stripped their buildings themselves often with taxpayers' money. All eyes are on Chase.

The human cost of Armley cannot be measured in monetary terms. Entire families have been wiped out. In July 1993 David Young, who grew up next door to the Armley factory, was dying of asbestosis. His mother and father had already died from asbestos related diseases. David was the last survivor of thirteen victims who had filed against T&N. Neither David or his mother had ever worked in the factory and he was determined to get to court, even with his oxygen mask attached to his face, to fight for justice. He died five months later, his final ambition denied him.

The company T&N has been estimated to be worth about £1.2 billion with stock market shares in February 1994 at an all-time peak. The last word on Armley goes to them. An internal, strictly confidential memo reads,

"Public access to the information that we have could explode a bomb that would wreck T&N."

Wittenoom

One of the most popular characters on the television screen in the 60s and 70s was a bearded Australian man who sung songs about kangaroos, a man with three legs and a sad song about two little boys. He was the ultimate light entertainer. Not only did he sing, he also sketched cartoons, painted pictures and played strange musical instruments. The words didgeridoo, wobble board, lagerphone and stylophone (the perfect Christmas gift!) all bring only one name to mind. Rolf Harris.

One thing most people seem to remember about Rolf Harris is his painting. With a few pots of paint and a large paintbrush he would transform a large blank piece of canvas into a picture in the space of two minutes, teasing and tantalising his audience as he worked. Humming and talking he would casually draw a painting of squiggles and lines. A final couple of blobs of paint and—hey presto—there was the picture.

Rolf Harris wasn't always an entertainer though and as a young man in 1948 he went to work for the summer in a mine. A blue asbestos mine. Wittenoom.

The town of Wittenoom is in the extreme north west of Australia about 1,600km north of Perth, just beyond the Great Sandy Desert. It is a hot, dry desolate place. And it was rough. Like the old wild west of America, Wittenoom was a tough town. When they weren't working the men drank, gambled and fought. Then they drank some more, gambled some more and fought some more.

"It was the law of the jungle," remembered Rolf. "They were a real bunch of desperados, fighting all the time. They had no mercy."

Rolf had gone to Wittenoom for summer holiday work. He was on a break from university and thought he could earn some money at the mine and do some painting. Unfortunately it was so hot that, whenever he tried to paint, the paint dried as soon as it hit the canvas. "It must have been 120 degrees . . . you had to drink water all the time, eat salt tablets. The men slept naked in the tents, that's how hot it was."

The mine shafts where most of the men worked were only three feet high and miners would be bent double throughout their shifts. Rolf said, "The first time I walked into the mine, I crashed into the roof and knocked myself out. You were working in these tunnels so low you couldn't straighten up. There was dust everywhere . . . around the shed where they crushed the asbestos, it was like a grey-blue haze. It was murder."

Luckily for Rolf he didn't have to work at the mine for any longer than three months. He was also lucky to get out of mine work. "Eventually the man I was shovelling the rock with said he wouldn't work with me any more because I wasn't pulling my weight. Thank God for that. I was transferred to laying water pipes."

Yampire Gorge, near the small town of Wittenoom, was the blue asbestos seam which was opened as a mine by Lang Hancock in the late 1930s. By 1940 the mine had produced 364 tonnes of blue asbestos which Hancock sold to an English asbestos company. The Colonial Sugar Refining Company (CSR) joined forces with Hancock in 1943 and the partners set up a new company to run the mine—ABA (Australian Blue Asbestos). The John Manville corporation of America soon became their biggest customer.

Wittenoom became a boom town and workers were recruited from Australia and all over the world. At the end of World War II in Europe, immigrants flocked to Australia for a better life. Many of these, mainly young men, ended up in Wittenoom. Hundreds of young Italians, Spaniards, Germans, Dutch, Yugoslavians, Poles, Hungarians and Greeks worked in the mines at Wittenoom. Most of them were teenagers or in their early twenties, young men trying to build a new life for themselves after a long hard war in Europe.

Up to 500 people worked at the mine at any one

time but, because of the appalling conditions, more than 8,000 men had been employed there at one time or another. Half of those 8,000 were made up from young immigrants who were told by CSR before they left Europe how good the conditions of work and the pay were and how nice the climate was.

In reality however, working conditions at the mine were primitive. There was a 500% turnover of workers in some years because most people wanted away from the place as soon as they got there.

The work was hard. Asbestos was torn out of the hills by hand, trampled into jute sacks by hands and feet and transported to ports by horse and cart.

In the mill where raw asbestos was grounded down to fibres one worker remembered how 100 watt bulbs looked like candles and you had to be within a couple of feet of someone before he was recognisable. The mill eventually got an extractor which didn't work. It blew dust outside into the air covering offices and lawns.

The mine itself was hot, dusty, dark and, until the 1960s, had no air shafts. Men crawled on their knees—it was impossible to stand up. Faces were caked with dust, in the 'food shack' men ate their meals off tables covered in raw asbestos dust and even used stringy blue asbestos fibres as dental floss.

The men at Wittenoom were never warned of the dangers of asbestos. In fact, like other factories around the world, they joked and played with it. "We used to throw handfuls of the stuff at each other for fun." They even used the air hose to blast dust into each others faces.

Professor Eric Saint, a twenty-nine year old graduate of medicine from Durham University, went to Wittenoom in the summer of 1948. He was horrified at what he saw. "It was hideous, absolutely hideous. There were no amenities, people were still living in tents and shacks. There were fights and mayhem going on everywhere."

To the Public Health Department in Perth, Dr Saint reported the barbaric medical facilities where wounds went septic because of filthy dressings and a filthy orderly. He also reported the dust which hung like a cloud over the entire area. His early examinations of the men also showed that many of them were suffering from diseases of the chest. He warned the mine managers about the dangers of asbestos and he repeatedly wrote damming reports to the Public Health Department. In one of his early reports, written in 1948, Dr Saint warned that,

"ABA will produce the richest and most lethal crop of cases of asbestosis in the world."

Dr Saint was one of the few professionals who tried to help the people of Wittenoom and he later went on to become one of the most highly respected and distinguished professors in Australia. He died in 1989.

However even after all the warnings of an epidemic of fatal diseases from Dr Saint, the owners of the mine did nothing to make conditions better or to protect their work-force. Instead CSR chose to cover up the real facts about asbestos then later denied all responsibility for the deaths of their workers. The trade unions and the health departments did nothing.

Vermiglio is a small village in the Italian Alps.

In the early 1950s, nine young villagers set off for Australia on a great adventure. Arriving at the mine by aeroplane, the pilot's main navigational aid was a blue-grey asbestos plume which shot into the air. When the young men saw what they had arrived at they were shocked. One later said, "we thought we were in Hell."

Over 1,000 Italians passed through Wittenoom and many returned home to their native land several years later where they married and raised children. But a deadly blue legacy went home with them. In the 1970s, all over Italy, ex-Wittenoom miners began to sicken and die.

By 1989 of those nine young men from Vermiglio five were dead or dying because of asbestos and one had been blinded by an underground explosion at the mine. In the small farming area of Abruzzi, 21 'Wittenoom boys' became ill. Gino Casale, one of four brothers who went to the mine, was concerned when two of his brothers became ill and urged them to get a medical examination. "Something is going on," he wrote. "All the boys of Wittenoom are dying."

But it wasn't just the boys who were dying.

In 1979 Joan Joosten was dying of mesothelioma. She had worked at Wittenoom as a secretary in the 1950s. She sued CSR and lost. CSR claimed that when Joan had worked for them mesothelioma was an unknown disease in the medical profession. So CSR were not to blame. Joan Joosten's appeal was set up for March 10th 1980. She died thirty minutes before it began. In a letter written by her husband just four days before he said,

"We will never be sorry we took on CSR and hope the next one who does will have an easier task."

The town of Wittenoom was actually fourteen kilometres away from the mine. It was a normal small town. Tailings (crushed rock from the mine) were supplied free to anybody who wanted them. They were carted around the town by truck and used on roads, the airport, the school and on the driveways of homes. In all over 30,000 tonnes were used in the town.

Great big pillars of dust would spring up ('willy-willies' they were called) in the town, sometimes right over houses where families lived. Children played in the dust, men came home from the mine covered in dust, women washed clothes covered in dust. The everyday fabric of home life was riddled with blue asbestos.

Asbestosis and mesothelioma killed mothers and fathers. The 'children of the dust' grew up with the word mesothelioma hanging over their heads. They knew exactly what it meant. And they are still growing up.

The mine closed in 1966. The first case of asbestosis had appeared in 1946 and the first mesothelioma in 1961. CSR were sued in 1977 for the first time but the victim died before getting to court. By 1986 three hundred people were suing. The Wittenoom death toll, by 1989, was 600. Across Australia the publicity of Wittenoom's deadly dust drove men and women, some only in their thirties, to their doctors. They wanted examinations and they needed reassurance. "I grew up in Wittenoom," they would say.

The mine at Wittenoom is now abandoned. A sign bearing a skull and crossbones marks the spot. Children are warned not to play there. The area is off limits.

When the wind blows in a certain direction blue tailings from the old mine are carried down the gorge to the town. When it rains flood water flows down to the Millstream—a main water supply of the Pilbara mining towns. Tourists and visitors can buy blueish souvenirs at Wittenoom to take home with them. There are no warnings, no danger signs, just pretty fluffy blue-black souvenirs.

It is estimated that more than 20,000 people have passed through the mine and town of Wittenoom. At least 2,000 of those people will be dead by the year 2020 because of their exposure to the lethal blue asbestos—asbestos which was transported across the world indirectly exposing untold tens of thousands of men, women and children. Entire families have been wiped out across the globe. In Vermiglio the village cemetery has been renamed by the locals. They call it Wittenoom.

Even as recently as 1973 and 1974 blue asbestos was still being used in Australian power stations. By a cruel twist of fate asbestosis took the life of Rolf Harris's father who had worked in one of those power stations. Rolf told me,

"My dad died of asbestosis in 1980 due, they think, to a period about forty years earlier when the large turbine broke down in the electricity power station where he worked. For about a month they had the stand-by turbine going while they repaired the big one, and the alternate one ran very ragged, shaking the whole place day and night.

"All the best water pipes were lagged with asbestos cloth and dad said going to work was like walking into a thick grey fog every day. Later in 1979 he got a bad persistent cough and was very short of breath."

Wittenoom asbestos found its way into docks around the world, power stations, trains and was even used in gas masks made in England in the 1940s. Think of all those people who have been unknowingly exposed—thousands and thousands of people.

On 4th February 1989, Val Doyle, a forty nine year old wife and mother, died. She was the sixth member of her family to die because of the asbestos of Wittenoom. Before she died she said,

"They have committed genocide on my family". Wittenoom has been called Australia's industrial Belsen.

Steve McQueen in Papillon, *1973*

5

The Movie Star

The Great Escape is one of Steve McQueen's best
known and successful films. Clydeside Action of
Glasgow have a poster from that movie on their wall.
It shows Steve McQueen on a motorcycle. Scrawled
across it are the words 'no escape from asbestos'.

Steve McQueen was born on the 24th March 1930
in Indiana, USA. He never knew the father who
walked out on him when he was a few months old.
And his teenage mother, who craved fun and
excitement, regularly left him with other relatives
while she went off to find bright lights and dancing.
He was practically raised by his grandmother and his
womanising uncle. The unstable child grew up to be a
dark, moody rebellious teenager and the teenager grew
up into a mysterious stubborn moody man.

After spending some time at Boys Republic, an institution for wayward boys, Steve joined the Merchant Marines. After jumping ship he took (and lost) several dead-end and uneventful jobs. Always looking for a scam Steve would sometimes steal in order to survive or just to prove he was smarter than the next guy. He often said if he hadn't been an actor he would've been a criminal.

At the age of twenty one Steve joined the New York City Neighborhood Playhouse and his career as an actor began. He began doing bit parts on stage and in 1956 appeared in his first movie, *Somebody Up There Likes Me*. He was paid $19 a day and the star of the film was Paul Newman. Over the next couple of years Steve appeared on television, on stage and in films but it was the 1958 TV series *Wanted: Dead Or Alive* which caught the public's imagination and catapulted him to stardom.

More films were offered to him and his name began to creep up the credits to top billing. His percentage share of the 1974 film *The Towering Inferno* (which also starred his longtime rival Paul Newman) and his salary grossed Steve over $12 million. By the end of the 70s Steve McQueen was the highest paid actor in the world.

In 1978 Steve caught pneumonia and was ill for a long time. It didn't seem to shake off and he developed a cough. He caught colds frequently afterwards. In January 1979, when shooting began on a new film, the cowboy western *Tom Horn*, Steve was still feeling under the weather.

During the weeks of filming he became tired and

breathless but he never let anyone on the set know. The first assistant director of the film was Cliff Coleman and his wife was a nurse. Steve bombarded her with questions about lung diseases—what was pleurisy like? etc. Doctors could find nothing wrong with Steve and decided that he had fungus on the lungs. The cause was possibly damp sea air. So, in response to this advice, he left his beach home for a ranch in the drier conditions of Idaho.

In the summer Steve had a lung biopsy and in September he began working on what would be his final movie, *The Hunter*. The first scenes to be filmed were stunts on top of a subway train. Steve refused to stand aside and let a stuntman do them and, even though he was ill, insisted on doing them himself.

Watching *The Hunter* on video in early 1994, I quickly become aware of how old Steve McQueen looks. He was only forty nine but he looks over sixty. In one scene he chases a teenager across a roof. His body is not agile and I got the feeling he was in pain. His back looks slightly hunched and many of his movements appear stilted.

Robert Relyea, one of Steve's friends, saw *The Hunter* at a Californian movie theatre when it opened in 1980. He hadn't seen Steve for a couple of years and was shocked at the image projected on the big screen. Robert was alarmed and deeply distressed about the way Steve moved. Clearly there was something very wrong and Robert realised Steve was trying to cover pain.

Steve developed an uncontrollable cough and became more and more breathless. In December 1979 he checked into a Los Angeles medical centre for tests. The test results confirmed that Steve had meso-thelioma. He told his daughter Terry not to worry as it wasn't a terminal disease, he didn't have cancer. "I'm going to make it," he said.

Steve had a passion for cars. He was an excellent driver and loved to race against the pros. Asbestos is found on the brake linings of cars and in the helmets and equipment drivers use. He would also have been around asbestos in some of his early jobs when he worked at construction sites and when he was in the forces.

In 1947 seventeen year old Steve McQueen had joined the Marine Corps and spent some time stationed in the Aleutian Islands. On one occasion when the facility was being visited by a general Steve decided to made himself a snack. He heated a can of beans on top of a tractor engine. Unfortunately the can exploded and splattered its contents over everything and everyone. Steve's punishment was six weeks in the brig where he was assigned to work in the hold of a ship. The engine room, which he had to clean, had pipes covered in asbestos linings. The men were in the process of ripping out the linings and replacing them. The air was so thick with asbestos particles that the men could hardly breath.

The ships of the US navy were in fact riddled with asbestos, as were the ships of the British navy. Even the Queen's ship, the Royal Yacht *Britannia*, had to have asbestos removed from it in the 1960s. In 1994 an ex-member of the Queen's staff who had worked aboard the Royal Yacht died of an asbestos related disease. All ex-staff of the ship were immediately recalled for medical checks.

Over the next few months Steve McQueen tried every treatment available to him including chemotherapy, radiation treatment and interferon, a new expensive anticancer drug. Nothing worked.

Only his close family were told that Steve had mesothelioma. His first marriage to Neile Adams had lasted sixteen years and the couple had two children, Terry and Chad. Ali McGraw, his co-star in the 1972 film *The Getaway*, became his second wife in 1973. They divorced in 1977. On 16th January 1980 Steve married for the third time. His girlfriend for the past few months was Barbara Minty, a successful model, and his wedding to her was a low-key casual affair.

Some of Steve's friends resented Barbara—they saw her as a newcomer. Over the next few months Barbara showed her mettle by standing by her husband to the bitter end.

Together his family conspired to keep the press at bay as rumours raged through Hollywood. "Steve McQueen has cancer, he's dying," was the word on the street. Steve himself denied it all. Neile and Ali lunched with journalists and talked about the virus Steve was beating. An American magazine published an article about the hopelessness and doom of McQueen. Threatening to sue, Steve reacted angrily and replied that he didn't have terminal cancer, he had terminal fury.

Desperate to find a cure for mesothelioma Steve tried unorthodox treatments. He tried a nontoxic cure for cancer (or so the so-called Washington doctor who discovered it claimed!) of nutritional therapy. This consisted of a diet of organic fruits and juices, vitamins, no junk foods only specified health foods. It didn't work.

He started calling up and visiting old friends. Still he refused to acknowledge that he was dying. If his friends asked if he was sick or had cancer he would say that it was all lies, he was fine. However his body was rapidly deteriorating. He was losing weight. His cheeks became sunken, his coughing got worse and breathing became more and more difficult.

Barbara nursed him while he attended San Fernando Medical Center for chemotherapy. They lived in a motor home behind the centre because Steve, who wanted his privacy, would have been recognised had he actually gone into the hospital. He didn't want the press to know what was going on.

When *The Hunter* was released in July critics slammed Steve's performance. "Tired daredevil" was how one newspaper put it. What they didn't realise at the time was that they were watching a dying man. Three days after the premiere Steve and Barbara drove to Mexico where Steve checked in for some very unorthodox treatment. Desperately clinging to hope and trying desperately to cling to life Steve McQueen, a multimillionaire, tried yet again to find a cure for mesothelioma. Time was running out.

The Plaza Santa Maria Clinic in Tijuana, Mexico was run by the same unorthodox doctor who had 'discovered' the nontoxic cure for cancer Steve had previously tried. In fact Doctor Kelley was actually an ex-dentist. He had been suspended from practising dentistry and was cited in Texas for practising medicine without a licence. He moved to Mexico.

The treatment Steve was subjected to included special diets, coffee enemas, vitamins, cattle cell injections, shampoos and massages, psychotherapy and prayer. Steve did not use painkillers but relied on prayer. He told his friend, Elmar Valentine he would take the pain—every single bit of it—even if it killed him.

To make matters worse he developed allergies to some of the medication. Night after night he would lie awake in agony. He would rant and rave, complain and throw things at Barbara. And he would cry. The only people he would allow near him were Barbara, Neile, Terry and Chad. He refused Ali's requests for her to visit him. Neile sadly told friends that it would be better for them to remember him as he was as they wouldn't recognise him now.

She tried to get him back to the States to a proper hospital. He refused. An old friend, Don Gordon, even thought up a plan to kidnap Steve using a helicopter and guns!

In the meantime the vulture press descended on the clinic. The going rate for a photograph of the very ill Steve McQueen was $50,000.

As his condition grew worse Steve decided that he'd like to spend Christmas with his family all together. Then, realising that he would not see Christmas, he told Neile to forget the whole idea. "I won't be here," he said.

After all the denials, on 2nd October Steve issued a joint statement with his doctors. It stated that he had cancer but that he was responding to treatment. Steve said,

"I say to all my fans and friends, keep your fingers crossed and keep the good thoughts coming. All my love and God bless you."

Through this apparent recovery the clinic received a lot of media attention. Dr Kelley insisted that some of Steve's tumours had disappeared, that new ones were not appearing and that those which were left were becoming light, like 'cotton candy'.

On 24th October Steve and Barbara drove home to their ranch in Santa Paula for a rest. His daughter Terry visited him there.

"He wasn't afraid of dying," she said. She was deeply saddened at the amount of pain her father was in and was proud of how he fought it. "He fought it up until the very end," she said.

In the meantime Barbara nursed him, put up with his fits of anger and depression and, in response to a friend saying it must be tough for her, sadly answered, "You wouldn't believe it."

Steve grew weaker. He couldn't breath. For the first time he started taking morphine to ease the pain. The tumour in his abdomen had caused his stomach to swell up. The clinic doctors wanted to operate on this abdominal 'dead tumour' as they said it was putting pressure on his internal organs. American medics warned that his heart would not withstand surgery. However Steve decided to go through with the operation and returned to Mexico.

On 6th November 1980, at the Clinica de Santa Rosa in Juarez, Steve McQueen underwent major surgery. A five pound tumour was removed from his abdomen. There was another tumour attached to his liver, his entire intestine was covered in cancer and his right lung was completely cancerous. He survived. He opened his eyes, gave the thumbs-up and said in Spanish, "I did it."

In the early hours of the following morning Steve had a heart attack. Then he had another. Then he died.

Newspapers across the world printed stories about Steve's death and, perhaps due to the intensely private way the McQueen family had handled the situation, many reported incorrect facts. There was one story of a five pound tumour being removed from his neck and another stated that he had died on the operating table. The word mesothelioma was rarely mentioned and instead the press reported his death as being caused by cancer.

The Standen family: (l to r) David, Alice, George, Dick (front) father, John

6
The Standen Family

THE STANDEN FAMILY. John and Alice Standen had four sons—John, George, David and Richard (known as Dick) and two daughters, Eva and Alice.

In the 1940s John Standen worked for Newalls Asbestos of Washington, Tyne & Wear as a lagger. He was sent out on contract work and lagged pipes and boilers in factories and buildings around the country. One after the other his sons left school and each spent some time working alongside him before going off to find other employment as laggers or pipe-fitters.

After a long day's work John and his fellow workers would go home to their families, usually still wearing their dusty overalls and white clad dusty shoes. John's daughter-in-law Pat told me, "As T & N did not provide cleaning services for the men's overalls, we had to wash them ourselves. I washed Dick's overalls every week. Dick told me some of the men quite often would wear theirs until they practically fell off."

John Standen suffered from thrombosis and died, aged fifty six, of a heart attack. At the inquest of his death, asbestos was named as the factor which had killed him. His death was followed by that of his daughter Eva who died of cancer in 1957. She was thirty six. Then, in the 1970s, three of the Standen brothers, one after the other, became ill from asbestos related diseases.

During the Second World War the four Standen boys joined the navy. John was killed when a troopship he was on was torpedoed off the Italian coast. George, David and Dick survived their wartime experiences and George was the first of the brothers to get married. His war bride was Betty, a local girl.

When the war ended David went back to civvy street and continued his working life as a welder. He worked with asbestos as part of his everyday life and travelled the world. One of his jobs took him to Malaysia where a huge power station was being built. As an asbestos expert, David taught the local Malaysians how to handle and use asbestos.

On one of his trips home to the UK his ship docked in Italy. A Danish co-worker and friend of his was met at the dock by his sister Else who had travelled all the way from Denmark. David and Else got on well together and, after going home to England to see his family, David went to Denmark to visit his friend—and Else.

"David came to Denmark a few times," Else said. "I also went to England to see if I liked it. We were bring married. I couldn't speak English!" Their wedding took place on April 20th 1957.

After being demobbed from the navy after the war, Dick met his future wife Pat. They married in 1952. Dick was the first of the three brothers to develop an asbestos related disease. Pat tells the story.

"Dick worked with asbestos right up until he died. In an early job he mixed up asbestos in buckets and put it over pipes and boilers. He worked in different factories in different boiler rooms. When our kids were young he even worked in a convent."

In 1971 Dick began to sicken and lose weight. He would travel home at weekends from his job and on one occasion became very annoyed at one of his sons.

"I knew he wasn't right because he was cross with one of the boys and it really hurt me. It just wasn't Dick at all. He loved his boys. He wasn't the kind of man to make a fuss. If he was ill he'd just go off on his own until he was better. Once he broke a bone in his hand and had to wait a couple of days to get it X-rayed because it had all swollen up. He got up next morning and went to work. In those days if you didn't work you didn't get paid so he went to work. He nearly passed out. But he didn't like a fuss. That's what he was like."

"Dick was taken to hospital and after only a week he was operated on. Then when he was well enough he came home. He had fluid drained from his lungs. He was not well but there was nothing they could do for him. I was told the lining of his stomach was covered in small growths and he had a large stomach tumour.

"The Monday before Dick died he was taken into hospital to have more fluid drained off. This was five months after he first went into hospital. He was so thin his bones stuck out. They opened him up and stitched him back up again. There was nothing they could do."

Dick died the following afternoon. He was forty six. Pat, at forty two, was a widow with four young sons.

"It affected the boys. None of them really knew that their dad was bad. I didn't really know myself. The doctors didn't know . . . or said they didn't know. I hadn't told the boys how serious Dick was because nobody really knew how long he would live. I had just told David, my eldest son, the weekend before as I didn't think it could be much longer. So David said he would stay home from work. He was only 16. The other three boys were at my mother's.

"I had phoned the hospital and they said Dick was sitting up having a fight with his lunch . . . he was winning or the lunch was winning. He was constantly sick after eating and had been all through his illness. I went shopping and I was going to visit him in the afternoon. It all happened so fast."

Else said, "Dick and David were so close . . . they were like twins. Dick was such a shock. I couldn't face him. We hit it off straight away. Very well. We would all; Pat, Dick, us, all the kids would go away all together. It was just such a shock. Then George was another shock."

In 1978 George became ill. He developed pleural mesothelioma and suffered for fifteen months. Pat said, "Fluid was drained from his lungs. It seemed to be an awful lot."

Sometime in 1978 David hurt himself while playing badminton. "Oh hell, I've busted a muscle," he told Else. At least, he thought he'd pulled a muscle. He had a pain in his side. Else continues the story.

"After a week the doctor said that it wasn't a muscle. He sent David to hospital for tests and scans. It was autumn 1978. He was clean. There was nothing on X-rays or anything.

"He was in pain all winter. He was fed up working, working, working and wanted to let us have a bit of a rest. It never dawned on me.

"David worked right up until two days before he went into hospital on Wednesday 8th March 1979. It was the last test they could do. To operate. On Thursday afternoon I went to visit. I hardly recognised him. When the surgeon came in I was called out. They were to operate on Monday but the surgeon said, 'I cant wait. I have to operate right away.'

"There was nothing in his organs. All clean, nothing on the lungs, nowhere. It was growing in the intestines, between them, like big fingers. One of them burst when he played badminton.

"The doctor said there was nothing they could do. He knew David was a very clever man and he said, 'I must tell him because he is too intelligent a man not to be told.' David was exceptional, with his brain and his hands. He was always reading. He built our house. He didn't really want to know. He had never been ill. He knew what had happened to Dick.

"George was getting injections and David thought, 'Oh well, perhaps they've found something they can do with the asbestos.' He still thought he could survive.

"In three weeks I took him home. Myself. There was an ambulance strike. In five weeks he died, in our home which we built ourselves. It was good that I could do that for him. They wanted to put him in a hospital to die but I said 'no thank you'."

In Copenhagen Else had trained as a nurse for newborn babies. She had spent some time nursing in hospitals and so her experience helped her cope with her very sick husband.

"I just got on with it. I didn't think about it. But it was very hard work. I didn't sleep at night. He needed medicine, morphine, every three hours. If it is not your husband you look after then you don't do it. In eight week he was only skin and skeleton. To see them go to nothing . . . you just don't think it is possible".

"It all happened so quickly," Pat said. "It seemed as though if they had been opened up it acted faster."

George, in hospital and completely unaware that his brother was ill, died the same day. David didn't want George to know he was ill. David had told Else, "Keep that away from him. Give him my love."

David died on the 2nd May 1979 at 11.45pm. George died eight hours later on the 3rd at 8am. Betty received a telephone call from the hospital telling her that her husband had died.

Else telephoned Betty to tell her of David's death and Betty then called Pat. As Betty and Pat talked, the hospital was trying to get through to Betty with the news of George's death.

Because Pat had lost her husband Dick just a few years before, the Standen family tried to shield her from the illnesses of George and David. "I didn't know exactly what was going on," she said. "They shielded me a lot from it all. So I only got bits of information years later."

When Else tried to claim against her husband's employers, T&N blocked everything. They denied all knowledge of David, even denying that David Standen had ever worked for them. T&N claimed that all their records were destroyed during the war. Luckily Pat found an old tax record belonging to Dick and through this Else was able recover information from the tax office which proved where her husband had worked.

The legacy of asbestos meant a fight for Betty Standen. The doctor refused to mention asbestos on her husband's death certificate. T&N also denied all knowledge of George. His case was dropped but later reopened by his son (who happened to be a doctor). Chase-Manhattan, the large New York based company who are currently suing T&N themselves, provided the family with relevant papers so they could fight— and win—their case. "The trial took place in October 1993 with the findings given in March 1994, six months later," said Pat. "The judge, who had never dealt with a compensation case like this before, did a very good job," she added.

But the story of asbestos wasn't over yet. A friend of Dick's, who emigrated to Canada, is now suffering from an asbestos related disease. He worked alongside Dick. A cousin of the Standen family is now suffering from asbestosis. He worked in the dockyards. Several of Dick's ex-supervisors have died over the years—all from 'cancer'.

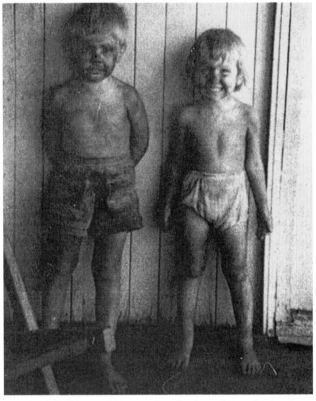

Two of the children of Wittenoom who have been playing in deadly blue asbestos tailings which were dumped around the town

7

Children of the Dust

THE PHOTOGRAPH. Two children standing side by side. On the left is a boy aged about six years old. On the right is a little girl, she looks about four or five. The girl smiles brightly, the boy looks unsure.

They both look blond but its hard to tell because of the dirt they're covered in. It's in their hair, on their faces, probably in their mouths. They are both barefoot and wearing only a pair of shorts. The dirt is all over the skin of their bodies, their chests, legs, hands, feet, knees and mum or dad is going to have a hard time scrubbing the muck off them in the bath tonight.

They look like normal kids who have been having a great time getting as dirty as possible. They are normal kids. It's the dirt they're covered in which is abnormal. It contains blue asbestos dust. These are two of the children of Wittenoom—children of the dust.

The family. The parents are Philip and Esther. The children are Virginia, Shirley and Val. Philip got a job at Wittenoom and in 1953 his family moved out west to join him. The girls were teenagers and Val, the youngest at thirteen, remembered the dust well— the entire town had a constant blueish haze over it.

"What I remember most from those early years was the heat, the bloody heat," she had said. "It was scorching. On top of that there was dust everywhere around the town from the tailings they used to dump. It was on the driveways, it was on the roads, it was on the basketball court. If you fell over you got filthy. It was in your eyes, your hair, all over your clothes."

Virginia, Shirley and Val grew up in the town and eventually they all married local men. In time some members of the now extended family moved away from Wittenoom to Perth.

In 1970 Philip died of asbestosis. Within six months Esther died of mesothelioma. Three years later asbestosis took the life of Val's husband and this death was followed by the deaths of Shirley and Virginia's husbands Frank, who died of bowel cancer, and Eddo, who died of asbestosis and cancer.

Five members of the family were now dead because of the dust of Wittenoom. In 1989 the sixth member to die was Val. She had gone to the town as a child and had played in the dust. The asbestos fibres which got into her lungs when she was only thirteen had caused mesothelioma to develop thirty six years later, killing her at the relatively young age of forty nine.

There was no escape from the dust for the children of Wittenoom. It was in the air, on people, on clothes, in homes, offices and in school. When the local school playground received free tailings from the mine to fill in potholes Dr Saint was horrified to see children sitting digging in it. Two of those children who dug holes in the playground died when they were still in their twenties.

In poorer countries children were (and are) used as labour in the asbestos mines. In South Africa in the 1940s children as young as twelve were discovered to have serious heart damage. They worked at a blue asbestos mine and their job was to trample down asbestos fibres into sacks before the raw material was shipped abroad. The doctor who examined these children did not expect them to live long enough for mesothelioma, lung cancer or asbestosis to develop.

From these mines raw asbestos was shipped all over the world. Dockers in the shipyards unloaded the stuff and unknowingly carried dust home to their wives and children. Raw material went into asbestos factories where it was made into products. Men and women worked it with their bare hands and again carried dust home to their families.

John Kennally's mother worked at the JW Roberts factory in Armley and she always came home from work covered in dust. John, a child, was exposed to raw asbestos. He died in 1988, aged only forty two, from mesothelioma. Another Armley child victim was Nellie Kirby who also died at forty two from mesothelioma. Her father would come home from the factory in his dusty overalls and hug his children or bounce them on his knee. Both parents of Arthur Slater worked in the factory. They would hug and cuddle their son as soon as they came home. Arthur died in 1980 from mesothelioma. He was sixty eight.

The workers came out of the factory covered in dust. It was in their eyebrows, hair and all over their clothes. They went home and left a trail of dust in their houses, all over their carpets. The factory itself bellowed its lethal dust all over the town and children in the streets played in it. It was all over the school playground.

Trudy Phillips is a good natured lady who's now in her 60s. Two years ago pleural plaques were discovered on her lungs.

Trudy
"I was born in Washington, County Durham where there was a chemical works and asbestos plant belonging to Turner & Newall. The houses and back streets were covered in white dust and we had a house directly opposite the factory. My father and brother worked there.

"But as children we all played amongst all this dust. There was also a very large, what we called, a 'pulp heap', which was all waste from the factory. We played on this too. Our shoes, I remember, were covered with this white pulp which hardened.

Dad and my brother had to shake their clothes and overalls in the back yard, after finishing a day's work . . . not that it made much difference to our home as everything was covered in white dust.

"I didn't leave there until I was nineteen years

Trudy Phillips (sitting) with her sister Edna. The girls grew up beside an asbestos factory in Washington, Tyne & Wear

old to be married. I had three cousins and two uncles who died of 'lung cancer'. They too all worked in the same factory. Masks were never thought to be needed. My father also died of 'lung cancer'."

Trudy now uses a nebuliser three times a day and finds her disease very difficult to cope with. From being very active she can now barely get off a bus.

"Sometimes I break down. It's just because I can't do the things I used to do. It's unfair . . . you're healthy all your life and now, when you should be enjoying retirement . . . this."

As a child Trudy had been a tomboy who enjoyed the rough and tumble of play. "We used to run up and down the pulp heap. Great fun," she told me. She also clearly remembers her uncles and cousins dying of 'lung cancer'. "They couldn't breath and we tried to open windows to let some air in but, of course, the windows and ledges were all white dust. It was everywhere."

In housing estates people live with asbestos every day of their lives. In 1991 over sixty families were evacuated from their homes in a council estate in Portsmouth. Air and soil samples taken at the area were found to contain asbestos. The houses had been built by the council on the site of an old naval rubbish dump.

In London in 1977 a piece of derelict land which was right next door to a nursery school was found to have sacks of asbestos lying on it. The sacks had been torn or ripped open and asbestos had spilled on to the ground. To stop curious children from getting close a piece of rope was put up while the asbestos was removed. Young kids stood at the rope and watched in mild amusement as, a few feet away from them, men in space suits 'safely' removed the dangerous material.

Asbestos is in the fabric of many school buildings—in the lagging on pipes or in the amosite tiles on the canteen ceiling. Fiona is now a lawyer and remembers asbestos being removed from her school in the 1970s. "We were all marched outside," she said. "It's really quite frightening."

Janet Smith was fourteen when, in 1976, a routine school X-ray showed up a scar on her left lung. She lived with her father on a council estate in south London. The ceilings of the block of flats where they lived were riddled with blue asbestos. Vandals, probably teenagers themselves, had torn the panels apart and pieces of fluffy dust were always all over the corridors. It was estimated that more than 200 men, women and children had been exposed.

Just this year in Armley, local resident Irene Merrill saw a group of workmen pulling apart a house. "They were throwing things out the window. There were kids everywhere. We have been warned not to disturb any dust . . . to be careful . . . and here are these men. I explained to one man how dangerous it was, not just for himself but for the kids playing around. He was very nice, very apologetic. I don't know if I got through to him. People just don't understand."

Workmen, even the professionals, can be very careless. I talked with one lady whose son was an asbestos removal employee. She said, "I've told him to be careful but you know what the young are like.

He's twenty-odd. He's a bit careless."

In 1979 some gas masks were stolen from a worksite at Ruchill Hospital in Glasgow. They belonged to workmen who were removing blue asbestos from a derelict building. The masks contained high density filters which, the police believed, would have blue asbestos in them. Children were blamed for the theft (no doubt they enjoyed playing with the masks).

War Babies

During the war thousands of gas masks were issued to the civilian population of Britain. In 1942 a special feature was introduced into some—blue asbestos filters. It was thought that the fine fibres of blue asbestos would help protect the wearer against the latest German poison gases. When children were evacuated from the main built up areas of the UK they were sent off to rural communities. They were allowed to take a bag and they had to take their faithful gas mask.

Margaret, now in her 60s, was evacuated when she was eight years old. She remembered, "It was great fun, a big adventure. But the gas masks were terrible. They made this sucking noise when you tried to breath with it on, you couldn't talk properly."

The factory where the masks were produced had their own epidemic of mesothelioma in the 1980s as former employees (mainly women) began to die. One of the scientists who developed the new masks said, "We all thought we were saving lives. None of us had any idea we were killing people."

The 'rag stores', as they were known in Glasgow were waste processing factories. Sadie worked in one during the war when she was sixteen. It was a dirty job. The factory was on three floors and each floor was connected to the one below by chutes. Waste was pushed down the chute where it went into a big container. Two girls would jump into the container, trample down the waste as much as possible and jump out. Then big crushers crushed and bailed the waste.

"They processed everything," she told me, "paper, cardboard, rags, cloth, string, ropes, you name it. It was a filthy job. We were covered in dirt, muck and dust. We put our own scarves around our heads—you could just see two wee eyes peeping out—and rags tied with string around our feet. We were always absolutely filthy. I used to have a bath at night when I got home and the water was black."

The rag stores processed waste from other factories around the Glasgow area including asbestos rope and sacks—from the shipyards. "They had great big ropes from the shipyards. They were on the ground floor where we used to eat our pieces [sandwiches]. We ate amongst filth and dirt and there were rats everywhere," she said.

Another worker was Robert who also remembered the filth. "The place was hoaching with rats. It was a dirty dirty place."

During the war years asbestos products were in high demand. The most logical place for disposal of those products was the rag stores—places where young teenagers like Sadie and Robert worked.

Sadie told me, "My friend Beth who worked with

me had a lung removed—I don't know why—then she died of a heart attack. Another pal, Chrissie, died quite young. There was something wrong with her lungs." Mary, another friend, is still alive but she suffers from emphysema of the lungs. The original building of the rag store has long since been demolished but the company are still in business. Sadie said, "They ruined my health. I worked there because my da made me. It was better money than anywhere else but I was just a kid—I was only young. I know I was exposed there. I know it." Sadie recently died of mesothelioma.

Over My Head

"I don't want to die like my mother," were the words of the daughter of another mesothelioma victim. "I saw what happened to her, you don't know until you see it. I will never forget what she went through. Never. All that pain." Lynn is in her twenties and she lives with the knowledge and the fear that one day she could develop the same disease that killed her mother.

"Mum worked in a factory and I used to go and meet her after school, I was about five, and we would walk home together. Every Christmas they held a party in the factory for the workers' children and mum always put my name down. Then when I got a bit older she started working a little bit longer and she used to take me inside to wait while she finished her shift. The girls she worked with were all nice and I would sit with some of them in the canteen. This went on for years until I was old enough to have a house key and go home by myself."

What Lynn didn't know was that the factory itself (which was not an asbestos factory) was riddled with asbestos. It was on the lagging of pipes, in corridors, in the canteen, in fact the dust circulated throughout the entire building. "I remember seeing white dust coating the corridors but I never thought anything of it. I just thought, it's a factory."

Asbestos doesn't care how old you are, what colour your skin is or what religion you are. All over the world children, who perhaps have watched their parents die, are growing up with the word, asbestos, over their heads. Even today in our near-21st century world people are still being exposed.

In India the T&N asbestos factory is probably being run exactly the same way as factories were being run in this country just twenty years ago. Another community, in a few years time, will find themselves facing an asbestosis/mesothelioma epidemic. No doubt a victims' campaign will spring up and the factory owners will move on. Another town, another country.

Figures from the Cancer Research Fund in England estimate that deaths in Britain from asbestos related diseases will peak in the year 2025. Mesothelioma has taken the lives of people in their twenties so people not even born yet could be amongst those statistics.

When I was a teenager I had a discussion with my mother. She told me not to use talcum powder "because it gives you cancer", she said. "Don't put it anywhere personal." Another conversation with a couple of friends at around the same time covered the same subject. One pal said, "I wouldn't put anything 'down there'. Yeuch!"

Now I know why talc was causing cancer. In 1993 a spate of cervical cancers in the south of England were blamed on talc laced with asbestos. How much of that talc was used on babies? An entire generation, now growing up, ready for the year 2025 ?

Asbestos is in the Earth's ecosystem and finds its way around the globe, carried by wind and sea. Even the unborn are at risk.

An autopsy performed in 1991 on a full term, still born baby found asbestos fibres in the child's lungs. The baby had never breathed a single breath by itself outside its mother's womb.

8

Rivers Of Tears

IN THE OLD days the river Clyde was the lifeline of Glasgow. Along its banks almost at the city centre the shipyards of Govan sprang up. Massive ships, such as the *Queen Elizabeth II*, were built here. The Govan docks housed over twenty shipbuilding companies and provided employment for thousands of men.

Glasgow was one of Britain's largest and most concentrated industrial areas and the shipyards were integral to the way of life. Young boys left school at fourteen and joined their fathers, uncles or cousins in the yards. In those days a job was a job for life and many of those boys left the yards when they retired at sixty five or when they were made redundant in the 1970s as the shipyards were wound down.

But in those days—in the decades of the 1930s

to the 1970s—sacks of raw asbestos arrived on these docks from abroad. They were unloaded from ships by dockers who would sometimes sit on the sacks as they ate their lunch—no masks, no protection. The men were never told asbestos was dangerous.

Some of the sacks made their way further east along the river to an asbestos factory in Clydebank. Inside the factory people handled the fluffy asbestos with their bare hands and, just like in other asbestos factories all over the world, they played with it.

In recent years Clydeside has been redeveloped. Blocks of new upmarket flats adorn the south side, the main rooms of which have stunning views of the city and the winding deep blue river. The shipyards are silent. Ships are no longer built here and the ghost yards lie quiet and empty. On the site of the old asbestos factory stands a gleaming new £180 million private hospital.

At first glance there seems, on the surface, to be not much trace remaining of this old Glasgow, and who is left to remember those old shipyards and the factories of long ago? Who can tell the story?

John McPherson worked in the Clyde yards. He remembers.

"Monkey dung. Did you know that's what it was called? It had asbestos in it. We used to mix it up. It was like dung, and we caked it on to pipes and stuff. It was used for insulating. It dried out. It was like a stukie, like on a broken leg. There was asbestos dust everywhere. If the light was right you could see it. It was like snow."

There was also asbestos 'snow' around the docks

of Hull, Liverpool, Portsmouth and Belfast and every other major port in the UK. Thousands of men across the country worked on these docks as thermal insulation engineers, laggers, engineers, dockers, joiners, pipe fitters, electricians, steel erectors, asbestos cladders and labourers. Most were never told that asbestos was dangerous.

At the end of the working day these men went home, wearing their dusty overalls, to their families. There are stories of wives dying of cervical cancer— cancer which some believe was caused by the husband transmitting asbestos dust to his wife through sexual relations. "He took it home to his marital bed," was how one sufferer told me of another. "It killed his wife." Yet again asbestos didn't just affect those directly exposed to it.

Dick Jackson was a lagger who worked for a firm in Hull. He first came into contact with asbestos in 1947 when he was insulating steam pipes and ship cylinders. He is now seventy years old and suffers from asbestosis. He has no idea when the next chest cold he gets might kill him. "I live with my fingers crossed", he said. In October 1994 Dick was diagnosed as having mesothelioma.

In 1970 Dick read a report about a company who were fined for not warning their employees about the dangers of asbestos. Since then he has been actively campaigning to get asbestos banned. He also helps other sufferers and their families, people like Marjorie, Leslie and Ronald.

Leslie Kipling was a steel erector and during his working years often handled asbestos. In July 1989 he started getting pains in his shoulders. Three months later he could barely move and his wife Audrey had to care for him twenty four hours a day—doing everything for him. Leslie died in February 1990, less than seven months from when he started feeling unwell. "He went downhill so fast," Audrey commented. "I live it over and over again in my mind." (*Hull Daily Mail*, June 1993)

People commented that something was wrong when Peter Higham stopped going to see his favourite football team playing matches. He never missed a game. Peter had worked with asbestos as a marine fitter for thirty years. In 1990 his weight dropped and he lost the strength to move.

"It all happened so quickly," said his wife Marjorie. "It was such a shock." Peter had a lot of trouble breathing and had a bad cough. He died in March 1990 and, like Audrey, Marjorie was left haunted by the memory of her husband's suffering.

Ronald Hoe was never told that asbestos was dangerous even though, as an insulation worker, he worked with it for over forty years. He wore an overall and made 'monkey dung' from asbestos and water with his bare hands. The air around him was full of asbestos dust. In 1982 Ronald discovered he had asbestosis and by 1993 he needed an oxygen supply by his side at all times and was confined to a wheelchair.

Dick Jackson has been actively campaigning for the victims of asbestos and travels the world attending conferences on the subject. One of his main goals is to get asbestos banned. "The country is spending millions of pounds on stripping asbestos out but is still importing the stuff," he says.

The 1990 international health and safety conference held in Copenhagen reported that only Norway, Sweden and Denmark had banned asbestos. In January 1992 the Hull Asbestos Action Group delivered the following petition to the British government imploring them to follow the Scandinavian policy.

"To the honourable the Commons of the United Kingdom of Great Britain and Northern Ireland in Parliament assembled, I wish to present the humble petition of Richard Jackson, the organiser/secretary of the Hull Asbestos Action Group and the humble petition of numerous residents of Great Britain, there being the massive number of 4,413 from the great city of Kingston-upon-Hull alone.

"The petition sheweth—a humble plea requesting the banning of all asbestos in Great Britain. Wherefore your Petitioners pray that your Honourable House might bring forth a Bill prohibiting the importation, manufacture and use of all asbestos in Great Britain, at the earliest possible date."

As yet no ban or announcement of a ban has been made.

As the incidence of men developing asbestos related diseases around the ex-shipyards of the UK increases, more and more people are discovering the real horrors of the magic mineral. Complacency is being replaced with sorrow, shock and anger.

Statements like, "We used to pull bits off the pipes . . . with our hands, I mean . . . bits of asbestos lagging. We never thought anything of it," are being replaced with, "They never told us. They never said a word, not a fucking word that this stuff could kill you. Now I know, I bloody well know and it's too fucking late!"

A forty eight year old ex-shipyard worker who wrote to me said,

"I have worked in the shipbuilding, oil and chemical industries all my life as a pipe fitter and a lot of the pipes I have worked with were lagged with asbestos. In the 60s working in Portsmouth Royal Navy Dockyard, nothing was said about asbestos being dangerous. We worked in asbestos filled engine rooms on ships and we were oblivious to what we were breathing.

"There are in this area a lot of asbestos related deaths of ex-dockyard workers and one ex-fitter, who I knew, died aged forty four."

Naval warships, submarines, giant ocean liners, even the Royal Yacht—they were all riddled with asbestos. As 'Brittania Ruled the Waves' with her magnificent British built ships, the men who went to war for Britain throughout this century were totally unaware of the deadly cargo in their engine rooms. Now, for some of them, the nightmare is only just beginning.

9
Dying with Dignity

I warmed both hands before the fire of life;
It sinks, and I am ready to depart.
                              Walter Savage Landor

"LIFE IS the most important thing. Don't waste a single minute." That's what my dad told me after my mother died. Like most people I've been to funerals, I've seen death but I had never really thought of my own death. Then I watched my mother die. She was a strong woman.

"I'm going to fight this thing. I'm not going to feel sorry for myself any more. I'm going to beat it," she had said. And she tried. She really tried. She was a strong woman.

There is one thing that every single one of us has in common. One day we will die. There are no maybes about it. It's fact. Most people, when asked how they would want to die, will probably answer, "peacefully in my sleep," or "quickly, without pain". Not one of us would want to endure months or years of agony.

How many of us ever really think about death? Our own death seems to be something that may happen many years down the line. Death is a subject that is rarely discussed particularly in Western society and yet it is an integral part of life. It happens all around us all the time.

My mother died with dignity. She kept her sense of humour right to the end and even with her body wracked with disease and pain she kept control of all her bodily functions—an incredible feat. She was a strong, courageous woman and we were very proud of her. Before she died my sister Anne told her so. And I was proud of Anne.

"No-one knows what I'm suffering. No-one should have to go through this." That's what she used to say. And, facing her own death she said, "If I need a painkiller—even if it kills me—I want you to give me it. I don't want to suffer. Okay? I don't want this pain. I don't want it. Will you do that for me?"

Should dying people be given painkillers to ease their agony? That question is faced every single day by the families of those who are dying.

The Wife
"My husband was in a nursing home suffering through the last agonies of cancer. I begged the nurse to give him more painkiller."

The nurse refused the wife's request stating that the husband had to wait another thirty minutes before his next dose of painkiller was due. The wife became hysterical and ran through the nursing home screaming and begging for someone to help her husband.

"I ran through the halls like a crazy woman. I couldn't stand what he was going through."

Luckily a male nurse came to her rescue and confronted the first nurse saying he was giving the painkiller to the dying man—and that was final. After sinking into a deep sleep the husband died during the night. It was a peaceful and painless death.

Euthanasia, taken from the dictionary, means the gentle and easy death, or the bringing about of such a death particularly in the cases of incurable and painful disease. The subject of euthanasia is a volatile one. There are groups around the country—VESS (Voluntary Euthanasia Society of Scotland) or EXIT—who believe in death with dignity. There are also groups such as LIFE who believe that life is of the ultimate importance and that no one has the right to take it away.

When Someone With Cancer Is Dying is a leaflet produced by Cancerlink. It answers the most commonly asked questions of the dying and of their families. One of the things it discusses is last wishes.

Last wishes are only as good as the people who carry them out. If someone really wants something then what's the harm? Perhaps they want to feel snow on their face or run barefoot through a field? Or to hear the words, 'I love you'. Life is for living.

When someone is facing death at the hands of a disease such as mesothelioma what goes through their mind? Steve McQueen started calling people from his past, old friends he had lost touch with on his rise to fame. My mother did the same. "I want to call Tommy in Canada," she'd say. Tom was her big brother.

People turn to their God. Perhaps it's a last ditch effort to save their soul or perhaps it's for comfort. People find comfort in religion and at the hands of death the most powerful being they have ever known is God. Totally ungodly people have found solace in their final hours.

Steve McQueen—the bad boy of Hollywood, a man who lived hard and fast, a man who loved women and fast cars, a complete and avowed atheist—turned to religion in the last few months of his life. In his final summer he started attending church on a regular basis. One of his oldest friends was astounded and commented that Steve had always described religion as 'bullshit'. Steve was protecting himself (or his soul) at all costs.

Terry McQueen was proud of her father, of the way he handled the pain of mesothelioma and of the way he fought for his life. "He wasn't afraid of dying," she said. "He was in a lot of pain. And he fought it. He fought it right up until the very end."

Steve died with dignity but his grieving family were in for a shock. After his death in Mexico his body was to be flown back to the States. As it lay on a slab at the funeral home someone took a photograph of it. This tactless and distasteful picture of Steve's naked corpse was printed across the world thereby causing his family even more distress and denying Steve McQueen, in death, some final dignity.

Mesothelioma strikes quickly. Of all the asbestos related diseases it is the one which gives the victim less time to survive. Sufferers of asbestosis and other cancers may have more time to live but they must learn to cope and come to terms with their illness. Asbestosis can affect the victim for over twenty years.

Coping

John McPherson found it hard to cope. After his operation for cancer of the larynx where his voice box was removed, losing the ability to speak had a devastating effect on him.

"I was what's known as a character," he said. "No party was complete until I arrived. I was the entertainment. I told the jokes." In his grief he turned to drink.

"I used to sit at my window in the morning watching people go to work and I'd think they were poor messins. I'd have my glass of whisky, my can of Guinness and my *Daily Record* and I'd watch them. I thought I had it made. I went mad. I don't know how my wife put up with me but she did."

"I withdrew into myself. I'd go to the pub and there was all this noise. Somebody was playing a machine. You'd be playing the jukebox and there'd be men arguing and talking loud. I couldn't handle it. I was always talking louder than anyone else so it never bothered me. Now it did. I couldn't make any noise."

"Pals would come up and ignore me and turn to whoever I was with and go . . . (here John makes words with his mouth and no sound comes out). Or they'd whisper. Or they'd shout dead loud as if I was deaf. I'm no deaf."

John couldn't handle being silent and he couldn't

handle the change in behaviour of the people around him. "I was totally out of control. One time I pulled my trousers down in the middle of the pub . . . showing off my bum!"

He went to a speech therapist to learn how to talk again. Although the voice can never be the same again, laryngectomees can learn how to speak using a hole in their neck. When he first started to talk after many months, John's pals and drinking buddies were amazed.

"One day I was sitting in the pub with a pal and another pal came up, ignored me, and started talking to him about me. It was like, 'how's John then?'. So I turned and answered him back. He got a shock. 'How did you dae that?' he's saying. So I told him I've got a wee button there on my side. He believed me!"

Realising he had a real problem with drink John joined Alcoholics Anonymous. He is now a spokesperson for them and he goes to meetings to talk to people and to give speeches. He told me, "I don't care who you are, where you've come from, but if you've got a problem I just treat everybody the same. I've been there and I know what it's like. People realise that. I'm now a spokesperson for the AA and chairman for youth unemployment centres in the Glasgow area. And I've set up this centre." (Scottish Association of Laryngectomees)

Coping with the diseases of asbestos can be a very lonely experience for sufferers. Most people don't realise what an asbestos related diseases is or what it means.

"People think I have asthma," Trudy Phillips said.

"They don't understand I can't do the things I used to do. Just walking up the street is hard. I used to run up and down the stairs of a castle delivering messages to people not that long ago and now I can't get off a bus. I feel so degraded. I used to be so active. I think people are staring at me."

Most sufferers and their families want to know the truth about their illness but many are kept, by the medical profession, in the dark.

"I thought asbestosis meant curtains," Nicholas McKenzie said. Like so many others Nicholas just wanted to know how long he had left. Months? Years? Decades?

Whenever I asked any doctor about how long my mother had left to live I usually got a vague meaningless reply. "Its hard to say," or "It depends," was the usual response. Never once did I get a straight answer—at least not up until her final week of life and by then it was pretty obvious how long she had .

Talking to other sufferers or their families can sometimes ease the burden and it can help to know that others understand. Only those who have been touched by an asbestos related disease can really understand the trauma, the hopelessness and the fury behind it. It is hard. Very hard.

10
The Victim
& the System

The Medical Profession

In 1991 a young woman named Anne Grant wrote down the story of her mother, Margaret McNair, who took ill at her home on the night of Sunday 14th April 1991. In contrast to my own mother, Margaret did not receive any comfort or help from the medical services. In fact the system ignored her. It's not a one-off—many sufferers do not receive the care and attention they need and many of them are never told what is wrong with them, even if the doctor knows or suspects.

Margaret, a sixty eight year old woman, spent the night of April 14th 1991 in agony. She couldn't breath. The next morning her concerned husband called out her local GP who sent her to the Royal Infirmary in Glasgow for tests. She spent almost two hours lying on a hospital trolley in a corridor. Five hours later she was finally admitted to a ward.

Over the next few days Margaret had tests and X-rays and fluid was drained from her lungs. On Monday 22nd, as she sat having her tea a doctor informed her she had lung cancer. Anne wrote, "Mum told by Dr X while she was having tea—no screens—no privacy—lung cancer—no treatment available." In this unprivate, abrupt manner she was also told there may be cancer in her womb and ovaries. By the time her family visited that evening they were all, naturally, very upset.

An ultrasonic scan of her ovaries and womb followed and on Wednesday 24th Margaret had developed pains in her chest and arm. Breathing was also very difficult. Her family were asked to leave and a nurse gave her a pain relieving spray which was administered orally. She fell asleep and woke at 6am the next morning. The pain had gone and she felt much better.

A new doctor from Belvedere Hospital took over her case and informed the family that the cancer was not in her lungs—it was surrounding them. The family thought this was good news and that Margaret would be 'good for a few years yet'. The tumour was progressing very slowly and she could go home soon, depending on the X-ray results. The doctor wanted her to return for a biopsy and to discuss possible treatment. "We were all very happy to hear this. Result of scan on womb and ovaries negative."

On Saturday 27th Margaret returned home. Anne wrote, "She could not even dress herself. Had to stop every few yards to sit down. Came home. Sat in chair all day—could not manage to get upstairs, had to be helped. Did not sleep all night."

By the next day Margaret's condition had worsened. She stayed in bed all day and was breathless. She made a confused call to her sister and returned to bed. By 10pm the emergency doctor had been called for. Margaret was by now in terrible agony. She had no painkillers. She couldn't breath. Anne arrived at the house as the emergency doctor, who said he'd left painkiller, was leaving. Inside the house Anne was shocked to find her father alone. He was trying to give his wife the painkiller.

"We entered house to find dad trying to half a tiny pill."

As Margaret's condition deteriorated the family tried desperately to get help from the emergency services. The doctor revisited but said there was nothing he could do. Margaret's breathing and pain got worse. At 4am on Monday 29th April 1991 Margaret died.

Fourteen days after being admitted to hospital, Margaret had been discharged and had died in immortal agony in her own house. None of the family had been told what was wrong with her but the next morning, through their GP, they discovered that the hospital doctor had suspected asbestosis.

The fiasco wasn't over for the family either. Shocked and grieving they had the officials to deal with. Police, doctors, the men from the mortuary and the procurator fiscal took several hours to sort out their paperwork. Margaret's body was eventually taken away at 2.30pm, almost eleven hours after she died.

In sudden deaths—and in cases where asbestos in involved—a report goes to the procurator fiscal. A postmortem may be asked for and, in relation to this, it is in the interest of the family to get the correct advice at the time of their relative's death. Clydeside Action on Asbestos strongly advise that ALL deaths due to asbestos should have a postmortem.

If the body of an asbestos victim is cremated and the family decide to sue those responsible for exposure in court, then they must have enough vital evidence to prove that the victim actually had asbestos in their body. In some cases biopsy results coupled with hospital records may be enough. The company who caused the asbestos exposure will deny all responsibility so families must be prepared to fight.

Margaret's death certificate states mesothelioma as the primary cause of death. No one knew, until a postmortem had been carried out, what had actually killed her. The family were left in a state of shock and anger. Anne wrote,

"Why did it take so long to discover what was wrong? Three years attending the Royal for tests, thyroid clinic then rheumatoid arthritis diagnosed.

"Why two different stories in hospital from two different doctors?

"Why released from hospital when obviously weak and unwell?

"Why could emergency doctors not do more for pain? Surely there is no need for someone to die in agony?

"Could the second doctor not offer some form of

painkilling injection or remove her to the Royal Infirmary? Instead of leaving a seventy two year old man (who was visibly distressed) alone without support?"

Margaret and her family, even though a hospital doctor had suspected asbestosis, were left in the dark. What they came up against was a wall—a conspiracy of silence.

When someone suffers or dies from an asbestos related disease the police, procurator fiscal, lawyers and hospital doctors all want to know one thing— where did exposure to asbestos take place? Victims and their families will find themselves trying to think back over as much as fifty years, to jobs they perhaps did as teenagers and have long since forgotten. If the sufferer has died the family are left with the knowledge that they may never know where their loved one was exposed.

Doctors themselves can do more harm than good. One particular doctor informed his patient, a lady named Mary, and her family that she had meso-thelioma. Right there and then—as the family spoke amongst themselves—he jotted down notes of what they were saying. The family didn't even realise what he was doing. Those notes became a rather biased medical report. The full story of the patient's previous employment was never discussed with the doctor. He just took it into his head to write down something and that something became a constant cause of contention to the family.

The worst part was that the family then had to continually fight against that one little sentence in the report—a sentence which the to-be-sued company jumped on. To them it was the perfect 'out' clause.

Some doctors are not on the side of the victim although they may well appear to be. Patients and families must be very careful about what they say. In Mary's case the doctor didn't even ask her about her work record.

In the case of my mum, if just one doctor had explained to us about asbestos and/or biopsies (articles about which have appeared in medical journals) I personally would never have allowed a biopsy to have taken place. It was as if they performed this so that they could write down something in their files. Without the biopsy would mum have lived longer? With it she had no chance. I will never forgive this piece of professional incompetence and deceit.

Court Cases
When it comes to court cases and company negligence the victim has to prove exposure to asbestos actually happened AND that the company behaved in a negligent way so as to cause exposure. The 'balance of probabilities' is a term widely used in the UK and what it means is that the victim must prove beyond reasonable doubt that they were exposed by a company who was negligent.

In America, however, the story is slightly different. In the US a victim only has to prove that there was asbestos in the workplace. There is no negligence factor and no balance of probabilities.

British court cases take a long time to prepare and prove and, as most people rely on legal aid to help them into court, the entire case must be sound before the legal aid board will allow it to get anywhere near a court. In Scotland the time limit for a family to sue a company depends on the life of the victim. Once a sufferer dies the family have a problem. Not only do they lose their key witness but on the third anniversary of the victim's death, the family completely lose the right to sue.

Witnesses. The other major problem. The family must find witnesses—people who worked with the victim—and these people have to remember seeing the victim and asbestos and the victim being exposed to asbestos. A difficult task, particularly if the event happened fifty years ago.

The companies sit back, drag their heels and wait for cases to be dropped as sufferers die and families stop fighting. That's what they want to happen. Before a case gets anywhere near a courtroom the powers-that-be will try to tear it apart and knock it down. They will use any piece of evidence or non-evidence to disprove the story—including comments from foolish, non-caring doctors who should have known better. The victims and their lawyers must fight tooth and nail.

One case of a few years ago concerned a worker who had been a foreman on a Clyde shipyard for many years. He was well known to many people who worked in the yards and he developed asbestosis from dust around the yards. When he tried to claim compensation the shipyard managers denied all knowledge of him and denied he had ever worked for them.

In Margaret McNair's case she had been exposed to asbestos before she ever met her husband. Her daughter Anne had to try to piece together the jigsaw of her mother's life from a time when she herself wasn't even born.

"Sometimes I just wish it was all over and I could get on with my life," Anne said. "But it doesn't go away. It's always there."

Most cases are settled out of court. The companies involved do not want attention brought to them—who knows what or who may come out of the woodwork. More former employees with chest complaints? Claims tend to get settled out of court—with secrecy orders or clauses attached.

In fact it's not the companies who pay. It's their insurance company. General Accident, Lloyds, Commercial Union, Royal Insurance, all the biggies of the insurance market—they all have 'asbestos' clients. Lloyds announced losses of £2 billion for 1991. In fact in the last four years they have lost over £7 billion.

Part of the blame for these losses are the huge payouts for asbestos and pollution cases in the USA. The 26,500 Names of Lloyds (the investors) have lost thousands of pounds, some have sued their agents for getting them involved and some have refused to pay up. One investor has lost £1.6 million—a sum he cannot afford to pay. Financial ruin has driven Lloyds Names to suicide.

The victims who do get into court have another obstacle in their way. The judge. In March 1993 an ex-joiner who worked on the QE2, won £43,000 compensation from Cape Building Products. Unfortunately he had to pay £6,000 of it back to the government. Clawback as its known is when the government takes back all the industrial benefits the victim has been paid as soon as the victim wins an amount in court. The joiner came out of court with £37,000, not a great deal of money for losing his health.

Industrial Benefits

Looking back, our family wasn't treated too badly (in comparison to most other cases) by the benefits agency. My mum got most of the benefits she was entitled to because I organised all her forms and made all her telephone calls. I'm used to dealing with people and asking the right questions. Computers and technical jargon don't scare me.

But what happens when an old couple become confused by all the paperwork? Many of the people who are now suffering from asbestos related diseases left school at thirteen or fourteen, as was usual back in the 1930s and 40s. They didn't get a complete education.

A lot of them are afraid of 'officialdom'—shiny new glass offices and young clerical staff who talk fast and type furiously into new fangled computer machines. All too often it is beyond them and many are confused and afraid. At the same time they are also coping with a very serious, life threatening illness.

Sometimes you may be lucky enough to find someone who will help you, sometimes not. In my investigations into places my mother worked at (and lived) I tried to find out if there had been any reports of asbestos through the environmental health offices in Glasgow. After all if anyone should know it would be them, wouldn't they? Do you think they'd tell me? Not a chance. "It's not on the computer". Wall of silence.

The Pneumoconiosis, Byssinosis and Miscellaneous Diseases Benefit Scheme was set up to pay an allowance to victims of industrial diseases. It covers various industrial diseases such as pneumoconiosis, asbestosis, silicosis, byssinosis, epitheliomatous cancer, carcinoma, mesothelioma and lung cancer. The scheme has different clauses and rules for different diseases and most asbestos sufferers fail to qualify for any benefit.

For her report *Victims Twice Over*, Joanne Lenaghan studied the cases of 412 people held at the offices of Clydeside Action on Asbestos. Of all the people suffering from an asbestos related disease, less than half of them were receiving Industrial Disablement Benefit. The members were suffering from the following diseases:

pleural plaques	67%
pleural thickening	65%
asbestosis	29%
mesothelioma	18%
lung cancer	7%

From these figures it is clear that most people had at least two diseases but most of them have been unable to claim industrial benefit because their diseases do not fall into the set categories of prescribed diseases as set out by the Benefits Agency which state the following:

pleural plaques not covered by the scheme:

pleural thickening—covered only if it is bilateral diffuse pleural thickening (pleural thickening

which is spread over the lining of both lungs) AND it
is accompanied by primary carcinoma of the lung
(cancer of the lung).

asbestosis—covered under the pneumoconiosis
clause but only if the sufferer has been directly
employed in asbestos handling or has been exposed to
dust in an occupation not listed in the rules. Asbestosis
is also covered if accompanied by primary carcinoma
(see pleural thickening above).

mesothelioma—covered if it is primary malignant neoplasm of the mesothelium of the pleura or of
the peritoneum (diffuse mesothelioma—spread over
the lining).

lung cancer—covered if the victim has worked
underground in a tin mine or has been exposed to
chloromethyl, methyl, pure zinc chromate, pure
calcium chromate or pure strontium chromate.

Asbestos is not mentioned.

The rules and regulations are more complicated
than set out here (see leaflet PN1 available from Social
Security offices) but what happens in real life when a
sufferer tries to claim? First of all he or she fills in a
form, sends it off and waits. Some time later the
Special Medical Board will arrange to examine the
sufferer.

The Board will then decide if benefit will be paid.
Joanne found that it usually takes over three months
for a decision to be made and most cases are turned
down. The average time for an appeal to be dealt with
was one year and five months.

The biggest obstacles in the way of sufferers was
the technical jargon qualifying all the rules and

regulations, satisfying prescribed occupation criteria and providing witnesses. The most successful claimants are mesothelioma sufferers, the people who have the least time left to live. The most unsuccessful are those with pleural plaques. Heart diseases, caused by asbestos are not even mentioned in the scheme even although it is known that fibrosis of the heart can occur many years before other symptoms appear.

On the books of Clydeside Action on Asbestos are people who worked in insulation, trade, construction, shipyards, engineering, factories and transport. There are also railyard, textile, office and school workers as well as electricians, cleaners, french polishers, plumbers, secretaries, teachers, bottle packers, asbestos weavers, munitions workers, and housewives.

A french polisher or a teacher is not a prescribed job. Neither is a housewife. Claiming industrial benefit is, again, a long hard difficult task. Most claims are turned down.

In reality very few asbestos related cases got to court. The emotional turmoil that victims and families go through means that trying to fight the system can become just too much to handle. Depression can easily set in and the feeling of total hopelessness can be very hard to get over. It takes a very strong person to keep going.

"Its like hitting your head off a brick wall," said the member of one family. "In our case we know where exposure took place, we have witnesses but yet we can't get a lawyer to take it up. It's crazy. We're running out of time and the company who did this committed murder and they are going to get away with it."

Doctors, companies, legal aid boards, courts, judges—sometimes it's as if the whole world is against you and it's not just individuals who feel that way. Entire communities have tried to fight the system.

In Eire in the late 1970s the Irish Development Authority helped the American owned company Raybestos Manhattan to build a £4 million factory in Cork. (In 1929 the Metropolitan Life Insurance Company in the USA found that half of the men working at the Raybestos (not Raybestos-Manhattan) and John Manville asbestos plants developed lung disease after working there for more than three years.) The Cork factory was to produce disc brake pads containing 25% white asbestos. The residents of Cork and nearby Ovens tried to stop it—groups of men and women carrying placards with EMPLOYMENT YES—CANCER NO and such stood outside the US Embassy in Dublin in 1977.

Ringaskiddy, a neighbouring town of Cork, was chosen as the dumping site for waste from the factory. The residents tried to stop the County Cork Council decision. They failed. The residents appealed. The appeal failed.

In response the Ringaskiddy Residents Assoc-iation picketed the dumping site and in May 1978 when Raybestos tried to dump asbestos they took along 25 policemen. 280 protesters, men, women and children, greeted them. Tempers flared, scuffles broke out and nine people went to hospital, one of whom was a ten year old boy who was kept in overnight for observation. Raybestos won.

Big companies, with all their money and

connections, are hard to fight. 'Everyone has their price' is an old saying and big multinationals appear to be able to buy anything and anyone they want.

In Australia the first successful case against the owners of the Wittenoom mine occurred in 1988. This was a blue asbestos mine yet it still took fifty two years from when the mine started operating, before one single person won a case.

All over the world since the start of this century asbestos companies have continually suppressed information, reports and documents which link asbestos and cancer.

11
Fighting for Justice

SUING THOSE responsible for causing exposure to asbestos is a long drawn out process. No-one will admit responsibility. These big company lawyers will drag their feet to delay any court action as much as possible. The reason is simple.

If they make it as difficult as possible to sue them, the sufferer will die by the time any court action is raised. Until 1993 after the death of the victim any damages awarded to a grieving family were a fraction of what the sufferer himself would have received.

However in 1993 the law in the UK was amended so that if the victim does die before any claim is successful, the family can still sue for the same amount. But it is still a difficult, time consuming process. The onus is on the victim to prove that the employer was negligent. Cases where there have been previous claims against a company are stronger.

But what happens if the patient cannot remember fifty years ago or where he or she worked. What if there are no other witnesses still alive? This is a problem many families have. It's no use being sure of where exposure took place—concrete evidence is needed. Companies may appear to have never been sued or original buildings and factories may have been raised to the ground.

It is a myth to think that because a person has an asbestos related disease they will automatically get compensation. They won't. Along with the pain, anguish and stress of illness there must also be a compensation fight.

Most companies, particularly those who have already been sued, prefer to settle out of court. They don't want court cases splashed all over the tabloids. They don't want to unnecessarily advertise the fact that they have exposed their workers to asbestos and this has been proven against them in court.

Those who have successfully gone to court have often ended up on the receiving end of a judge who doesn't understand the disease. Take the story of an old man who received just £16,000 compensation for asbestosis. The reason for such a low value on his health and life? He smoked. The judge practically told him it was his own fault. Perhaps the judge missed the point—smoking contributes to lung cancer but to develop asbestosis or another related disease, a person must have been exposed to asbestos dust or fibres.

The monetary values that companies place on life

varies. Margaret, a sixty six year old woman who was suffering from pleurisy, sued the Ministry Of Defence for £200,000 in 1993. It was settled quietly out of court. In 1994 the Ministry of Defence themselves sued Shipbreaking Industries of Motherwell for £16 million, claiming that the company had left a Faslane ship breaking yard polluted with asbestos. This case was also settled out of court.

Bob, an ex-shipyard worker, won only £37,000. In comparison to this in January 1994 a wren successfully sued the RAF for £200,000 because they fired her when she got pregnant. In April an ex-army officer was awarded £300,000 compensation because she had to resign her commission when she got pregnant. Thirteen years had elapsed but she still managed to sue. Asbestos victims have a three year time limit. Once three years have passed after the death of a loved one killed by asbestos, the family lose their right to sue those responsible.

A successful career is one thing but asbestos victims lose their health and their lives. The compensation, for the very few who do manage to get it, is blood money.

Nicholas

Every summer the Scottish town of Dunoon hosts the Cowal Games. Traditional Scottish events and competitions, such as tossing the caber and highland dancing, take place. The town is busy. Tartan and bagpipes are everywhere and beer tents quickly fill up with men in kilts.

During the August 1990 games one of the kilted

men in the beer tent suffered a heart attack. He was immediately rushed by ferry across the Firth of Clyde to hospital. It was a shock but the next day Nicholas McKenzie felt fully recovered. "I felt great," he said. "On top of the world".

An investigation by his doctor, who was a heart specialist, showed that his heart was in excellent condition. The doctor was puzzled. Nicholas was a very fit and agile man. One of his favourite hobbies was hill-walking (no mean feat in Scotland) and he'd often go off on his own up a mountain somewhere.

I met him in April 1994. He looks younger than his sixty four years, has a mop of white hair, clear blue eyes and, although he's thin but not gaunt, his cheek bones are clearly visible (a common sight amongst asbestos sufferers). As Nicholas and his wife Nan talked to me their two year old granddaughter toddled over to sit on her grandad's knee for a cuddle. This is a nice family, in a nice home. It's hard to imagine how asbestos could have touched them.

Two months after his heart attack in 1990, Nicholas started to feel a tightness in his chest and began suffering from headaches. He went back to his doctor. Nicholas and Nan wanted to know what was wrong but instead they came up against a brick wall. Earlier Nicholas had been prescribed heart pills which he had stopped taking. He asked to see a lung specialist. His GP was unhelpful and decided that the chest problems were all in the mind.

"They said it was my imagination and that I should see a psychiatrist. I did go for a while but I knew it wasn't my imagination."

Eventually he was sent to the chest clinic at a local hospital for tests and X-rays. One day, as the couple were leaving the doctors office, the hospital doctor vaguely mentioned asbestos.

"He asked me if I had ever worked with asbestos. It was like an afterthought, just as we were going out the door."

In fact Nicholas had fibrosis in his heart and it had been this—not coronary heart disease—that had caused his heart attack. In October 1991 chest X-rays showed that his chest was clear but one year later another X-ray showed that pleural plaques had formed on his lungs.

He said, "We tried to find out more. I would have taken over 3,000 heart pills for nothing by this time. I had to keep asking questions. If I hadn't kept going back we wouldn't have known about this."

Nan added, "They just shrug their shoulders and say, 'there's nothing we can do'. It was as if we didn't matter. We wanted to find out what could be done. We wanted information. The first thing one doctor said to us was, 'if you're thinking of claiming, forget it'. I couldn't believe it. We were concerned about his health not a claim. It didn't even cross our minds. I just could not believe a doctor could say that."

Nicholas contacted Clydeside Action who are trying to help him. "They gave me all these forms," he said. Like so many others Nicholas is trying to get industrial benefit under the Pneumoconiosis, Byssinosis and Miscellaneous Diseases Benefit Scheme. It's a long hard struggle. His medical papers have been misplaced on several occasions and his industrial tribunal, which has taken months to get prepared, was set for June 1994 (One year and eight months after pleural plaques were discovered on a X-ray).

"I used to get breathless once a fortnight, now its once a day. They say its not affecting me but it is. I used to go hill-walking on my own. I wouldn't do that now. I couldn't."

"I could live with this for another twenty years but I don't know what's happening. Do I have twenty years? No-one will tell me."

Nicholas is still fighting for benefits—he hasn't even begun a civil claim against the company who exposed him to asbestos and already he's finding out just how difficult it is.

Another victim who managed to live just long enough to tell his story is Willie Rigley. On April 3rd 1994 Willie had to give evidence to lawyers acting for the firm he was suing for compensation for exposing him to asbestos. He was so ill from mesothelioma the court went to his home. Willie, practically on his deathbed, was subjected to hours of questioning by lawyers. He died a few days later. He was forty six.

The story is a familiar one. In Australia in June 1977 the first case to be brought against the owners of the Wittenoom mine, CSR (now named Midalco), was instigated by Cornelius Maas, an ex-miner. The writ was issued but, less than two weeks later, Cornelius died.

In Scotland Clydeside Action are fighting for the rights of victims of asbestos. They want the companies responsible for exposing thousands of people to be ruined—not the insurance companies who pick up the tab—companies like T&N. "Those b******s should pay," they say. They also want a global ban on asbestos and a special hospice for sufferers of asbestos, "to stop the barbaric treatment of victims."

They have a charter which states that asbestos related diseases are at epidemic levels worldwide, that victims are denied diagnosis, state benefits are denied and that the whole process of claiming puts extra stress on the victims. They believe that human rights have been breached, many in the medical profession are in breach of medical ethics and that the state is guilty of the oppression of victims. They propose that asbestos should be banned, there should be a re-evaluation of criteria of the diagnosis of asbestos related diseases and a new ethical code should be put in place in the medical field.

These sound like strong words. They are strong words. And there is reason.

"We are all dying in here," Iain McKechnie told me.

The biopsy is another cause of contention. Biopsies reduce life expectancy and yet they are part of the routine in Glasgow hospitals. When biopsies are carried out, they are usually done with a long needle which goes through the chest wall into the lining or lung. However the tumour can progress down the needle track.

The Department of Social Security and Clydeside Action agree that biopsies do more harm than good and should not be carried out just to find out what is wrong with a patient. Hospital doctors however, don't seem to acknowledge this fact and continue to perform biopsies on patients without informing or discussing this with the families involved. Its the same old story—the professionals are trusted to know what they are doing.

The asbestos industry itself has, over decades, managed to advertise and push its products and has spent small fortunes making sure we all know that asbestos is safe. They even tell us that its the blue stuff that's dangerous—the rest is really okay.

The Health & Safety Executive have produced leaflets to tell us all about asbestos. One of them *Asbestos In Housing* lets us know that asbestos-cement is used in garages, sheds and cold water tanks. Sprayed asbestos is used in steel-framed houses and communal areas of flats. It is comforting to know that asbestos may be in our oven pads, ironing boards or heaters.

The HSE advice is simple. Asbestos is safe—do not disturb it—unless the product is crumbling. Don't cause dust and don't breath it. The advice for disposing of asbestos waste is to dampen it down, seal it in a strong plastic bag marked ASBESTOS and call your local council.

In complete contrast to this advice, the Australian Asbestos Diseases Society advise that if someone finds or suspects that they have found asbestos in their home they must immediately contact a qualified professional. Their message is—'Above all NEVER remove asbestos yourself'.

Julia was a cleaner who had worked in a school for over thirty years. Sometime in the 1960s her job involved cleaning a science lab. The ceiling of the laboratory was damaged and the insulation was exposed. Asbestos dust fell onto the worktops. Julia wiped it up.

By the 1990s Julia had developed chest problems which a consultant put down to fibrosis of the lung. Her claim that she had asbestosis (fibrosis caused by asbestos exposure) was rejected. Besides, the job of school cleaner does not come under the prescribed occupation clause.

Statistics

"Official statistics of deaths caused by asbestos related disease are far too low." This is a statement I have heard time and time again from different people in various asbestos campaigns. Are they right?

The official statistics for the Glasgow area in the years 1988 to 1991 are:

1988	1989	1990	1991	total
45	55	53	49	202

These figures are for males and females.

When Joanne Lenaghan did some statistical analysis on the members at Clydeside Action she found that, during 1988 – 1991, sixty people had died—30% of the above total. The members of CAA included in Joanne's statistics amounted to a few hundred people—not the entire city of Glasgow (which would have up to a million people). This would imply that the official figures are too low. Further research by Joanne Lenaghan also showed that even CAA figures were at least another 50% too low—making the official figures even worse.

Part of the problem is the inaccuracy of death certificates (up to 40% of which state the wrong cause of death). Coupled with this are the words 'asbestosis' or 'mesothelioma' which some doctors seem to fear—words they refuse to write down as a cause of death, using 'lung cancer' or 'cancer' instead.

Even a lifetime diagnosis of mesothelioma has become lung cancer, carcinoma, lung tumour or even heart disease on a death certificate. Postmortems can clear some of this up but, in Scotland, very few postmortems are actually performed. Only a postmortem will tell if fibrosis of the heart has occurred rather than coronary heart disease. Heart disease and cancer are, of course, the biggest killers in the UK. How many are asbestos linked?

Without that answer official figures have to be wrong.

The biggest killer in Northern Ireland is chest, heart and stroke illnesses, which kill approx 10,000 people every year. Coupled with this Belfast is also currently gaining in the asbestos related diseases death and illness statistics due to the town being an industrial and shipbuilding area. Is this just coincidence?

In the course of writing this book I would talk to sufferers about their asbestos related disease and, when talking about family members (apart from the asbestos sufferer) the words 'heart attack' and 'cancer' kept creeping into the conversation—time and time again. Another coincidence?

Of the official Health & Safety figures of deaths by asbestos related diseases in England and Wales, Dick Jackson of Hull Asbestos Action Group said, "Many cases of asbestos related diseases are not investigated. These official figures are far too low and do not report the true seriousness of the problem."

Death Certificates mentioning asbestos related diseases 1968-1988 England & Wales
(Health & Safety Statistics)

	1968	1973	1978	1983	1988
asbestosis & mesothelioma	201	300	499	694	961

For figures that are too low the above statistics show a frightening trend.

In January 1994 the Cancer Research Campaign, headed by Julian Peto, analysed the UK death by asbestos figures (up to 1994). Professor Peto was stunned at the results. Instead of an expected decrease in deaths in the 1990s, the trend was going up. He stated that, "asbestos is already causing more cancer deaths in Britain than any other industrial carcinoma."

He added, "It will be even worse in thirty years time."

Within the next ten years official deaths from asbestos are expected to triple.

12
The Future

"With all kind of cancer there is hope.
But not this one."

Else Standen 1994

MY MOTHER is dead. She was killed by asbestos. My dad was seventy years old in 1994. My parents should have been celebrating their Golden Wedding Anniversary in 1996. Instead my dad sits sad and alone in his house, surrounded by family photographs.

All over the world the story is the same. Old men have lost their wives and old women have lost their husbands. But this is not just a 'pensioners' disease'. It is on-going. In Australia young men and women, some barely out of their teens, have died in their twenties from asbestos related diseases. In England last year a thirty-six year old school teacher developed mesothelioma.

In towns like Armley and Wittenoom children were exposed to asbestos dust—dust which makes no distinction between a foetus in its mother's womb and an eighty year old man. Exposure can take place over decades or within a matter of moments. It makes no difference—there is no safe level of asbestos dust exposure.

Accumulated Immune Deficiency Syndrome, AIDS, has killed approximately 204,000 people to date in the USA and about 5,500 in Britain. There are millions of pounds being spent on advertising, education and research into the causes of this disease. Scientists compete with each other to find a cure. Hopefully one will be found. Movie actors, actresses, pop stars and even Royalty appear in public to spread the AIDS word and to make money for the charity.

There are no cures for the asbestos related diseases even though they kill thousands of people in the UK alone every year. There are no millions of pounds, no rich and glamorous stars drawing attention to the subject. The people who suffer from these diseases are ordinary, working class men and women. Most of them have worked all their lives, some of them did their bit during the war years for their country and yet they were deliberately exposed to a mineral companies and governments knew was dangerous. These people have been sacrificed, so that others could make a fast buck. The victims are left to cope on their own.

My mother didn't deserve to die the way she did. She did nothing wrong. She was brought up to believe that you should pay your own way in this world, be good to your family and friends and owe no debts. When she retired she bought her council house and made it comfortable for herself and my dad. A nice new shower, a new bathroom suite, a new kitchen. She wanted to enjoy her retirement and watch her grandchildren grow up.

But she was robbed.

There is not a day that goes by that I don't think about her. And I'm sad and angry. Very angry. This book was started because of her and, even as it's being written it breaks my heart. This is a book of tears.

Asbestos is a big, sad word. It's also an international disaster. And the whole sorry tale has, like dust, been swept under the carpet.

THE END

151

Appendix 1

Useful Addresses

Clydeside Action On Asbestos (CAA)
15 St Margaret's Place, Briggait, Glasgow G1
tel 0141 552 8852
Offers support and help to asbestos victims and their families. CAA also help to put sufferers and families in touch with each other. They are actively campaigning to abolish the idea that there are safe levels of asbestos and describe it as an 'uninsurable risk'.

Society for the Prevention of Asbestos and Industrial Diseases (SPAID)
38 Drapers Road, Enfield, Middlesex EN2 8LU
tel 01707 873025

SPAID was set up in 1979 by Nancy Tait. Send a large SAE for an information pack on asbestos, compensation, benefits and legal issues.

Hull Asbestos Action Group
123 Cambridge Street Analby Road,
Hull HU3 2EE
tel 01482 223287

Advice on any aspect relating to asbestos. Claims handling, disposal etc. Secretary, Mr Richard Jackson

Cancerlink
17 Britannia Street, London WC1X 9JN
telephone Information Line 0171 833 2451
MacLine (for young people affected
by cancer) 0800 591028
Asian Line (info & support in Hindi,
Bengali & English) 0171 713 7867
Cancerlink Scottish Centre, 9 Castle Terrace,
Edinburgh EH1 2DP
tel Information Line 0131 228 5557

Cancerlink provides information and emotional support to people affected by cancer. This includes people with cancer, their friends and families and those working with them. It also acts as a resource for local contacts and support groups.

Chest, Heart & Stroke, Scotland
65 North Castle Street, Edinburgh EH2 3LT
tel 0131 225 6963 fax 0131 220 6313
Scottish Regional Offices are in Inverness:
Chest, Heart & Stroke, Scotland
5 Mealmarket Close
Inverness IV1 1HT
tel : 0463 713433
fax : 0463 713699

& Glasgow:
Chest, Heart & Stroke, Scotland
103 Clarkston Road
Glasgow G44 3BL
tel : 041 633 1666
fax : 041 633 5113

also in Ireland:
Chest, Heart & Stroke Association
21 Dublin Road, Belfast BT2 7FJ
tel 01232 320184 fax 01232 333487

England & Wales
NOTE—for England & Wales CH&S is now the
Stroke Association. For lung and chest problems
contact the British Lung Foundation.

The British Lung Foundation
8 Peterborough Mews, Parsons Green,
London SW6 3BL
tel 0171 371 7704

leaflets available: *The Facts About Your Lungs*, *Asbestosis*, *The Way Our Lungs Work*. BLF also run a BREATH EASY club across the country for people with lung problems. There is also a free quarterly newsletter with updates and information.

The Voluntary Euthanasia Society of Scotland (V.E.S.S.)
17 Hart Street, Edinburgh EH1 3RN
tel 0131 556 4404 (24 hours)
fax 0131 557 4403

A society supporting the right to die with dignity and comfort.

Please note that all of the above charities are independent of each other and have no input into the contents of this book.

Appendix 2

References

Books & Reports

Asbestos Killer Dust (BSSRS Publications Ltd, 1979)

Blue Murder Ben Hills (Sun Books, Australia, 1989)

Lung Cancer—the Facts Chris Williams (Oxford University Press, 1992)

Steve McQueen—the Untold Story Of A Bad Boy In Hollywood Penina Spiegel (William Collins, Glasgow, 1986)

Medicines—the Comprehensive Guide (Parragon, 1993)

Wittenoom—the worst disaster (Asbestos Diseases Society of Australia)

Asbestos—what you should know (Asbestos Diseases Society of Australia)

Victims Twice Over Joanne Lenaghan (East End Management Committee,1994) available from Clydeside Action on Asbestos

Hull Asbestos Action Group (Reports 1990-1993)

Leaflets

The facts about your lungs—Asbestosis (British Lung Foundation)

The Way Our Lungs Work (British Lung Foundation)

When someone with cancer is dying (Cancerlink, 1991)

Life With Cancer (Cancerlink)

Voluntary Euthanasia—your questions answered (VESS, 1990)

PN1 *Pneumociniosis, byssinosis & some other diseases* (Benefits Agency, 1992)

Asbestos in Housing (Department of the Environment)

Mesothelioma Research Report (National Cancer Institute)

newspaper articles from

Chicago Tribune, Courier & Advertiser, Daily Express, Daily Mirror, Daily Record, Evening Courier, Evening Times, Glasgow Herald, The Guardian, Halifax Courier, Hebden Bridge Times, Hull Daily Mail, Mail On Sunday, Northern Star, Sunday Express, Sunday Mail, Sunday Post, The Times, Yorkshire Post.

Notes

Chapters 4 and 7—All 'Wittenoom' quotes are taken from *Blue Murder* by Ben Hills.

Chapters 5 and 9—All 'Steve McQueen' quotes are taken from *Steve McQueen—the untold story of a bad boy in Hollywood* by Penina Spiegel.